AUTUMN'S CATHEDRALS

A Pictorial Tour of Division 1-A College Football Stadiums

AUTUMN'S CATHEDRALS

A Pictorial Tour of Division 1-A College Football Stadiums

Jason Wolfe
and Stephanie Wolfe

Publishers Design Group
Roseville, CA 95678
1.800.587.6666

Library of Congress Control Number: 2002108193

Book and cover design: Robert Brekke

ISBN: 1-929170-07-6

Publishers Design Group
Roseville, CA 95678
www.publishersdesign.com
800.587.6666

Printed in China

DEDICATION

Many books are dedicated to family members, friends, and/or co-workers. Although my family, friends, and other loved ones are deserving of such an honor, I am going against the norm to lift up a much broader, but equally deserving audience.

This book is dedicated to all the men and women who lost their lives in the World Trade Center and Pentagon attacks. To the brave firemen, policemen, and civilian volunteers who so valiantly put their own lives on the line to save others, the doctors and medical personnel who worked unceasingly to help the victims, and to our men and women who take up arms to defend our country in the United States Military, (especially my brother-in-law Rex Laceby, a hard-charging Marine), thank you, and God bless.

A note on information and statistical accuracy: Due to the ever-changing climate concerning college football stadiums, it is almost a given that by the time this book is distributed, some of the information contained in its pages will be outdated. To the best of my knowledge, all information contained within is updated and factual as of May 2002.

A note on photography: Our original intent was to obtain photos directly from each school. However, late in the process of making this book, we discovered that not all were able to deliver publication quality photographs. Alternate sources were researched and images of many venues were acquired. Still, we were not able to obtain the best representation for some stadiums. For this we apologize.

CONTENTS

My heartfelt thanks to:

Jesus Christ: My personal Lord and Savior who has blessed me with so much more than what I deserve. Thank you for being my best friend and allowing me to engage in such an endeavor. I love you.

John and Stephanie Wolfe: Thank you for being the best parents anybody could ever have.

Rex and Shannon Laceby: Your love and support for me has been immeasurable. I couldn't dream of having a better sister and brother-in-law. Thank you.

Tyler Laceby: You're the greatest kid in the world and "Kuncle" Jay loves you very much.

Victoria Gable, DVM: God blessed me with a wonderful woman to share my adventures with. Thank you for opening your heart and life to me. You're an Angel, OK? :-)

Peter and Eiva Griffiths (Rah-Rah), Andy and Michelle Ware, Dave and Laura Ware: Your support from afar has been appreciated.

Phil and Nancy Ware, Alice Wolfe: Your love and acceptance of me has always been wonderful.Good luck with your own book Noni, though I know you won't need it. Grandma, we all love and miss you.

Don, Alice, and Brandon Gable: I love you all very much.

The South Carolina Gang: Thank you for opening your homes to me, and letting me ramble on about this crazy project. Aunt Susan, you make the best Breakfast Casserole.

Adam Wilson, Seth De La Riva, and Mike McCorriston (My Friends): You are the best friends a guy could have. Thank you for your support of me and for your great sense of humor. Mike, the Red Sox will win a World Series – I promise.

Paul A. Jongeward, Ed.D.: What a family friend you have been. I cannot put into words how thankful I am for all your help. What a man of God.

Athletic Directors, Sports Information, and Media Relations Personnel: Your help in putting this project together has been much appreciated. A special thanks goes out to Coach Vince Dooley, Athletic Director at the University of Georgia, for allowing me to spend the day with you before the Georgia-Tennessee game in 1998.

AUTUMN'S CATHEDRALS

Every Saturday in autumn, multitudes of people; young and old, rich and poor, gather in hallowed super-structures known as college football stadiums to watch their favorite teams play the greatest sport on earth. It has been this way since the late 19th century, when these modern day architectural marvels were then just a dream.

As college football entered the 20th century and as local and intercontinental rivalries first started to take shape, fans attended games in greater numbers. Great, charismatic, and magnetic college football figures such as Knute Rockne, Pop Warner, Red Grange (affectionately known as the Galloping Ghost), George Gipp, Amos Alonzo Stagg, Jay Berwanger, and Don Hutson carried college football and exalted it to new awe-inspiring heights never before imagined. This influx of attention set the stage for the mammoth stadiums that are now home to college football games every weekend.

Of course, there have been legendary players, coaches, teams, and crowds that have yet taken college football farther than their great predecessors of the early 20th century. Examples include: Army's Mr. Inside and Mr. Outside (Doc Blanchard and Glenn Davis), Ray Nitchke, Billy Cannon, Jim Parker, Ernie Davis, Jim Brown, Roger Staubach, Tommy Nobis, Dick Butkus, and Gayle Sayers. The coaching fraternity of the past seventy years is as legendary as the players. Red Blaik at Army, Frank Leahy and Ara Parsegian at Notre Dame, John Mckay and John Robinson roaming the sidelines of Southern California, Darrell Royal at Texas, Vince Dooley at Georgia, Frank Broyles at Arkansas and Bud Wilkinson and Barry Switzer at the University of Oklahoma are just a few of the all-time greats. Others include Bob Devaney and Tom Osborne at the University of Nebraska, Joe Paterno at Penn State, Bobby Bowden at West Virginia and Florida State, Coach Eddie Robinson at Grambling, and of course the greatest of them all, Paul "Bear" Bryant who coached at Maryland, Kentucky, and Texas A&M before finishing his legendary career at Alabama.

This book gives a firsthand look at the stadiums (all 117 Division 1-A teams) that allowed these great figures to thrill so many millions of fans. Moreover, this book will describe the great aura that surrounds these facilities. You will know why LSU is generally regarded as the loudest stadium in the nation. There will be information about Frank Howard's Rock at Clemson, the legendary Notre Dame Stadium, and the science project that ended up being what is now Husky Stadium at the University of Washington. Autumn's Cathedrals will also cover the 100,000+ seat campus stadiums, which reside at the Universities of Michigan, Penn State, Tennessee, and Ohio State.

This book has everything a college football fanatic would want to know concerning the facilities their favorite teams play in. These stadiums are just as much a part of the college football experience as the legendary pre-game tailgating traditions and the games themselves.

CLEMSON

DUKE

FLORIDA STATE

GEORGIA TECH

MARYLAND

NORTH CAROLINA

NORTH CAROLINA STATE

VIRGINIA

WAKE FOREST

Photo credit: Jim Carpenter

THE A.C.C.
(Atlantic Coast Conference)

The Atlantic Coast Conference is not known just for its great basketball programs. The ACC has always been steeped in rich football tradition with awesome players, legendary coaches, and magnificent teams. Long before the great Florida State Seminoles entered the conference, ACC teams were challenging for National Championships on a consistent basis.

Florida State, Clemson, and Georgia Tech have been synonymous with ACC football and National Championships for years, while teams such as Maryland, North Carolina, North Carolina State, and Virginia have gained great success, not only within the league, but on the national level as well.

These stadiums are as impressive as the teams that play in them. For a number of years, Clemson's Memorial Stadium and Florida State's Doak Campbell Stadium have been widely regarded as two of the loudest venues in the nation. The other ACC facilities, given their size, host just as vociferous and knowledgeable crowds as any across the land.

CLEMSON

Clemson Memorial Stadium (1942), Clemson, South Carolina

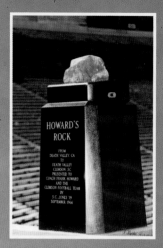

Steeped in tradition, Clemson Memorial Stadium is undoubtedly home to one of college football's loudest crowds. Erected for play before the 1942 season, Clemson opened Memorial Stadium by walloping Presbyterian College 32-13. Known as "Death Valley", a name given by an opposing team's head coach, the stadium was constructed in a valley, which had been previously inhabited by trees, bushes, and poison oak.

Unlike most college football facilities, Memorial Stadium has the distinction of being built by students and team players. It is even said that legendary Clemson coach Frank Howard, deposited a chew of tobacco in one of the four corners of the stadium while the concrete was being laid.

When completed, the not so friendly confines of Memorial Stadium remained untouched until capacity renovations began in 1958. Enlargements also occurred in 1960, '78, and '83. Another memorable year in stadium history was 1974, when the University renamed the football field in honor of coach Frank Howard.

Although the atmosphere in Clemson is extraordinary, the greatest legacy to Clemson sits atop a hill. "Howard's Rock", is rubbed by all Clemson players on their way down to the field before every home game, which sets up what announcer, Brent Musberger once dubbed as, "the most exciting 25 seconds in college football." Howard's Rock was brought to Memorial Stadium from Death Valley, California.

NICKNAME: Tigers
MASCOT: Tiger & Tiger Cub
PLAYING SURFACE: Natural Grass
SEATING CAPACITY: 81,473
CURRENT HEAD COACH: Tommy Bowden
NOTABLE PLAYERS/COACHES: **Players:** Banks Mcfadden, Michael Dean Perry, Levon Kirkland, Brian Dawkins, Rod Gardner. **Coaches:** Frank Howard, Danny Ford, Tommy Bowden.

Photo credit: Craig Jones/Allsport   Top: Clemson Athletics Media

DUKE

When one thinks of Duke University, the immediate response would be to their historic basketball program and Final Four traditions. But Duke is also home to an impressive football history as well. From the late 1930's to the mid 1940's, Duke's football team not only vied for conference championships, but displayed national contending football teams as well. They boasted a number three ranking in the AP poll in 1938, as well as a number two ranking in 1941.

Since October, 1929, the stadium, which is named after legendary football coach Wallace Wade, has become the Blue Devils home. Wallace Wade Stadium is a luxurious and comfortable venue for spectators to watch some of ACC's most exciting football. Though seating capacity is a modest 33,941, the facility is no stranger to hosting huge crowds such as the Duke-North Carolina game in 1949, when 57,000 spectators watched the Blue Devils win.

Historically, it has housed many great visiting and home teams, but none more dominating and ferocious than Duke's own 1938 squad. That year, they registered nine consecutive shutouts in nine regular season games on their way to meeting Southern California in the Rose Bowl. With 40 seconds left in the game, the Blue Devils were looking to cement another shutout, until the Trojans scored a touchdown to steal the game 7-3. Duke also hosted the first football game south of the Mason-Dixon Line in 1888 beating North Carolina 16-0.

The stadium was host to the 1942 Rose Bowl due to concern for player and fan safety. Games, which attracted large crowds, were suspended on the west coast during the beginning of World War II.

NICKNAME:	Blue Devils
MASCOT:	The Blue Devil
PLAYING SURFACE:	Natural Grass
SEATING CAPACITY:	33,941
CURRENT HEAD COACH:	Carl Franks

NOTABLE PLAYERS/COACHES: **Players:** Ace Parker, Ernie "Can Do Kid" Jackson. **Coaches:** Wallace Wade, Bill Murray, Steve Spurrier.

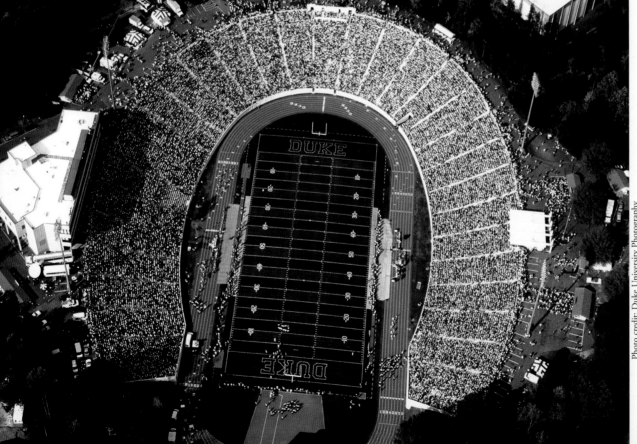

Photo credit: Duke University Photography

Autumn's Cathedrals   3

FLORIDA STATE

Doak Campbell Stadium (1950),Tallahassee, Florida

Florida State's Doak Campbell Stadium is one of college football's most feared places to play for opposing schools. Its name is taken from Florida State's first school president, Doak S. Campbell. The stadium offers spectators a taste of luxury as well as excitement and electricity every Saturday in autumn.

Built for the beginning of the 1950 season, Doak Campbell Stadium had a seating capacity of 15,000. Renovations in 1954, '61, and throughout the rest of the decade, raised seating to an impressive 40,500. Still more seats were added in the late 70's early 80's, and again in the 90's.

The stadium is, without a doubt, one of the nation's finest, boasting top of the line scoreboards and a luxurious press box. There is not a bad seat in the house and all who attend see the action without obstruction. The unique construction allows fan noise to be trapped within the facility. This, along with the incredible noise created by fans, is a major reason why Doak Campbell Stadium is regarded as one of college football's loudest sporting venues.

A legendary coach, great teams, and loud knowledgeable fans, help make Doak Campbell Stadium a must see for any college football enthusiast.

NICKNAME:	Seminoles
MASCOT:	Osceola
PLAYING SURFACE:	Natural Grass
SEATING CAPACITY:	80,000
CURRENT HEAD COACH:	Bobby Bowden

NOTABLE PLAYERS/COACHES: Players: Burt Reynolds, Fred Biletnikoff, Deon Sanders, Charlie Ward, Chris Weinke. **Coaches:** Bill Peterson, Bobby Bowden.

Photo credit: Ryals Lee Jr., FSU Photo Lab

Courtesy of Georgia Tech

GEORGIA TECH

Bobby Dodd Stadium/Grant Field (1913), Atlanta, Georgia

Bobby Dodd Stadium/Grant Field is home to the Yellow Jackets from Georgia Tech. This cozy stadium sits in the middle of Georgia Tech's campus in the heart of Atlanta. It takes its name from its legendary Georgia Tech head football coach who led the Yellow Jackets from 1945 through the 1966 season. During this time, Georgia Tech was always a conference and national championship contender. The field is named after John W. Grant, who gave the university the money to build the initial seats.

Construction began in 1913 when Georgia Tech students built 5,600 seats that comprise the West Stands. Though seating construction didn't start until that year, games on the present site of Bobby Dodd Stadium have been played since 1905. It has the unique distinction of being the oldest on-campus stadium in the nation. Due to its age, the structure has undergone many renovations throughout its storied history. From its original 5,600 seat capacity to its modern 46,000 level, the stadium has withstood construction and demolition in 1924, '25, '48, '58, and '62. In 1967, there were actually 58,121 seats, but in 1986 the construction of the William C. Wardlaw Center dropped capacity to its current level.

Despite the continuous ascending and descending capacity levels, this venue boasts top of the line electronic scoreboards and press boxes as well as new athletic prescription turf, which was installed in 1995.

Bobby Dodd Stadium also houses a statue of John Heisman, which stands on the north side of the playing field.

NICKNAME:	Yellow Jackets
MASCOT:	Buzz
PLAYING SURFACE:	Grass
SEATING CAPACITY:	46,000
CURRENT HEAD COACH:	Chan Gailey

NOTABLE PLAYERS/COACHES:Players: Bill Curry, Dorsey Levens, Joe Hamilton, Keith Brooking. **Coaches:** John Heisman, Bobby Dodd, Bobby Ross, George O'Leary.

MARYLAND

Byrd Stadium (1950), College Park, Maryland

Byrd Stadium is home to the University of Maryland Terrapins. Built in 1950 and named after Maryland's first legendary coach and future Athletic Director, H.C. 'Curley' Byrd, the second Byrd Stadium is a modern Olympic-style facility. The original stadium, built in 1923, became too old-fashioned for the rising football program and its fans.

In 1950, Byrd Stadium seated 34,800, but with the aid of temporary stands, could seat 50,000 spectators. Construction after the 1990, '91, and '95 seasons raised capacity to its current 48,055 mark. The Terrapins' first game in the facility was against rival Navy, September 30, which Maryland won.

Historically speaking, the stadium has been host to many classic moments. It has been home to great football players and coaches, creating exciting football teams. Playing in the friendly confines of Byrd Stadium, Maryland has won nine conference titles, as well as the 1953 National Championship.

Interestingly enough, Queen Elizabeth II adorned the venue to watch Maryland play North Carolina in 1957. Also of note, Paul "Bear" Bryant returned to the school where he received his first major collegiate head coaching job in 1974, bringing with him his Alabama Crimson Tide football team.

NICKNAME: Terrapins
MASCOT: Testudo
PLAYING SURFACE: Grass
SEATING CAPACITY: 48,055
CURRENT HEAD COACH: Ralph Friedgen
NOTABLE PLAYERS/COACHES: **Players:** Randy White, Boomer Esiason, Frank Reich. **Coaches:** H.C. 'Curley' Byrd, Paul "Bear" Bryant, Jim Tatum, Jerry Claiborne, Bobby Ross.

Photo credit: Doug Pensinger/Allsport

Photo credit: Flying Fotos-Chapel Hill

NORTH CAROLINA
Kenan Memorial Stadium (1927)
Chapel Hill, North Carolina

The Frank H. Kenan Football Center is where the University of North Carolina plays its home football games. It was built in August of 1927, and is one of the nicest facilities in the South. Frank Kenan and his family have made generous donations throughout the years, which helped build the stadium and the football complex.

The past few years, Kenan Stadium has undergone many renovations which has brought it up to par with the best stadium complexes in the nation. New and remodeled facilities, such as locker rooms and a luxurious press box, have elevated the beauty and comfort to the Kenan Football Center. The field has also been reconstructed to allow water to be soaked up through the grass, which keeps it in excellent condition. With the recent addition of 8,000 plus seats, the stadium's capacity is now at an impressive 60,000.

The last decade has seen a rise in enthusiasm for North Carolina football, which is partly due to the remodeling of its facility. This has undoubtedly helped in recruiting some of the nation's best talent.

Kenan Stadium is not only one of the ACC's nicest all-around facilities; it also is one of the nation's most picturesque venues to watch a college football game.

NICKNAME: Tarheels
MASCOT: Ramses
PLAYING SURFACE: Grass
SEATING CAPACITY: 60,000
CURRENT HEAD COACH: John Bunting
NOTABLE PLAYERS/COACHES: **Players:** Lawrence Taylor, Leon Johnson, Dre Bly, Ebenezer Ekuban, Julius Peppers. **Coaches:** Bill Dooley, Dick Crum, Mack Brown.

NORTH CAROLINA STATE

Carter-Finley Stadium (1966), Raleigh, North Carolina

Carter-Finley Stadium is the highly volatile and fan friendly home for the Wolfpack. It is named after N.C. State alumni and brothers, Harry and Nick Carter, and local philanthropist A.E. Finley.

North Carolina State University's football team has made major strides recently due to the addition of Head Coach Chuck Amato. Excitement is high in Raleigh and for good reason. N.C. State looks to expand on their impressive eight-win 2000 football campaign, and they hope to dominate in scenic Carter-Finley Stadium.

Dedication-game came against South Carolina, October 8, 1966, in front of 35,000 fans. The Wolfpack have an impressive home record in their 35 years at Carter-Finley, which will no doubt get better due to the caliber of players coach Amato recruits.

Carter-Finley boasts top of the line amenities, which include, a luxurious triple deck press box, and a contemporary lighting system. The Wolfpack also play on one of the nicest grass fields in the nation. The stadium is scheduled to undergo seating renovations that could put fan capacity at 70,000-seats.

NICKNAME: Wolfpack
MASCOT: Mr. & Mrs. Wuf
PLAYING SURFACE: Grass
SEATING CAPACITY: 51,500
CURRENT HEAD COACH: Chuck Amato
NOTABLE PLAYERS/COACHES: **Players:** Torry Holt, Lloyd Harrison, Koren Robinson. **Coaches:** Lou Holtz, Dick Sheridan, Chuck Amato.

Photo credit: Flying Fotos-Chapel Hill

Photo credits: Jim Carpenter

VIRGINIA
David A. Harrison III Field at Scott Stadium (1931)
Charlottesville, Virginia

In a conference full of magnificent stadiums, David A. Harrison III Field at Scott Stadium is no exception. Nestled on the University of Virginia campus with Monticello Mountain and the Blue Ridge Mountains in sight, Scott Stadium is both pretty and updated.

The stadium and its field take their names in honor of a couple of highly generous individuals, whose donations helped propel the University of Virginia football program to the top of the Atlantic Coast Conference. David A. Harrison III, the field's namesake and former U of VA alumnus, gave the Virginia athletic department a gift of over five million dollars, while Frederic and Elizabeth Scott donated close to $400,000 towards the upgrading of the stadium. For this, Frederic Scott asked that the stadium be named in honor of his parents, Robert Scott and Frances Branch Scott.

Scott Stadium opened for play in 1931, and has been the home for the Cavaliers ever since. It boasts a beautiful grass field, with a permanent lighting system, comfortable aluminum seats where spectators can take in the gorgeous Virginia scenery, and a luxurious press box. Located in the south end zone, is the immaculate Bryant Hall, which is one of the nation's finest multipurpose facilities, housing home and visiting locker rooms, training facilities, team meeting rooms, and a huge dining area which overlooks the field.

NICKNAME:	Cavaliers
MASCOT:	The Cavalier
PLAYING SURFACE:	Grass
SEATING CAPACITY:	61,500
CURRENT HEAD COACH:	Al Groh

NOTABLE PLAYERS/COACHES: Players: Bill Dudley, Tom Scott, Herman Moore, Chris Slade, Tiki Barber. **Coaches:** George Welsh, Al Groh.

WAKE FOREST

Groves Stadium (1968), Winston-Salem, North Carolina

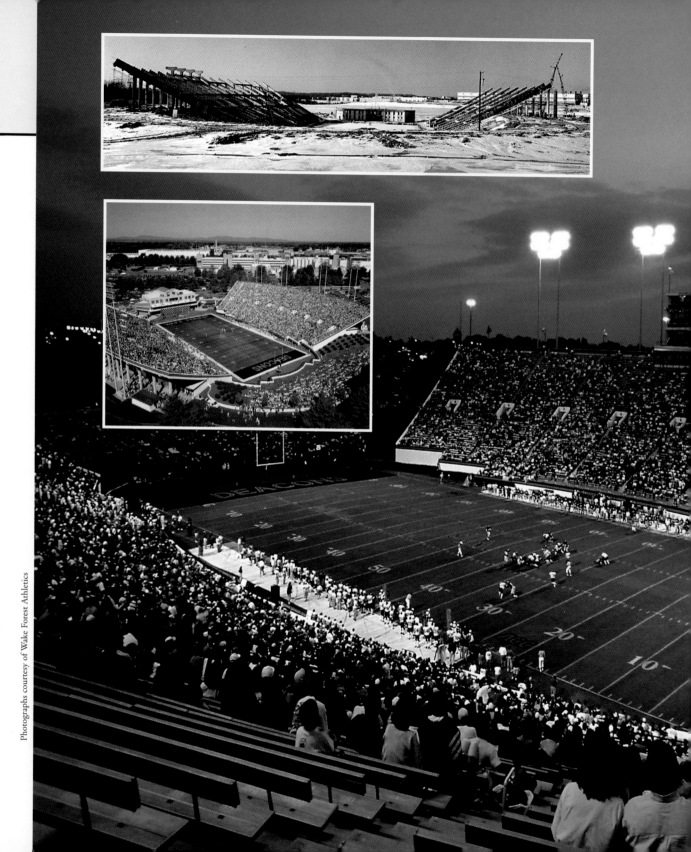

Opened in 1968, Groves Stadium has had its share of memorable moments. The facility is named after Henry H. Groves Sr., who made generous contributions for the construction of the stadium at the original site of Wake Forest University in Wake Forest, NC. When the school moved to Winston-Salem, Henry and brother Earl continued to make contributions to the school.

Groves Stadium is another in a long line of gorgeous ACC football venues that boasts many amenities that would make most schools envious. Some of these include, a state of the art electronic scoreboard system and a five-level press box. The magnificent press box is home to box seats, as well as a media area. At the north end of the venue sits the Bridger Field House, which houses new and refurbished locker rooms for home and visiting teams.

Wake Forest has had many successes at home, going undefeated a number of times. In 1979 they may have played their most memorable game against nationally ranked Auburn. Wake, after trailing at halftime 38-20, roared back to beat Auburn 42-38. This game marked the first time that two nationally ranked teams have played in the facility.

It is widely known that there is not a bad seat in the house. With new head coach Jim Grobe at the helm, there is no doubt that Wake Forest fans will fill Groves Stadium to watch a new and exciting brand of football.

NICKNAME: Demon Deacons
MASCOT: The Demon Deacon
PLAYING SURFACE: Grass
SEATING CAPACITY: 33,941
CURRENT HEAD COACH: Jim Grobe
NOTABLE PLAYERS/COACHES: Players: Brian Piccolo, John Mackovic, Michael McCrary, Ricky Proehl. **Coaches:** D.C. "Peahead" Walker, John Mackovic, Bill Dooley.

BOSTON COLLEGE

MIAMI

PITTSBURGH

RUTGERS

SYRACUSE

TEMPLE

VIRGINIA TECH

WEST VIRGINIA

BIG EAST CONFERENCE

Football played in The Big East Conference has a uniqueness all its own, with its wide-open play and hard-nosed style. Always rich in football lore, the Big East boasts some of the nicest and most luxurious venues in which to watch college games.

When one thinks of Big East Conference football, the teams of Miami, Virginia Tech, West Virginia, and Syracuse come to mind. Big East football provokes thoughts of historical programs such as Pitt and the up-and-coming teams, Temple and Rutgers. Conference stadiums, especially the Orange Bowl, have hosted some of the greatest football games in the history of the sport. These facilities have no doubt added to the incredible legacy started by its legendary players, coaches, and teams of the past.

An entire book could be written describing the great players and games, which the teams that now comprise the Big East Conference have had, and been a part of, but this book is about the stadiums, which have hosted those indelible memories. Still, it is no small task to aptly describe these wonderful facilities.

BOSTON COLLEGE

Alumni Stadium (1957), Chestnut Hill, Massachusetts

Alumni Stadium is the home to Boston College football, and is a beautiful and majestic place to be on an autumn afternoon.

A capacity crowd of 26,000 was present when the stadium was dedicated September 21, 1957, against Navy. Since that initial game, Boston College has enjoyed a great amount of success at home. Over the years Alumni Stadium has become one of the toughest places to play for visiting teams.

The facility is home to a number of modern amenities, which include luxury box seats on the east and west sides, as well as an electronic scoreboard system, and spacious press boxes. In addition, it boasts a great public address system, lighting system, as well as other outstanding features. One of its most enduring sites is the field on which the Eagles play. Sitting on the floor of the stadium is a beautiful artificial turf field, which only enhances the splendor of the entire stadium.

NICKNAME:	Eagles
MASCOT:	Baldwin
PLAYING SURFACE:	Artificial Turf
SEATING CAPACITY:	44,500
CURRENT HEAD COACH:	Tom O'Brien

NOTABLE PLAYERS/COACHES: Players: Doug Flutie, Bill Romanowski, Stephen Boyd, Matt & Tim Hasselbeck, William Green. **Coaches:** Frank Leahy, Jack Bicknell, Tom Coughlin.

Photo credit: John Quackenbos

MIANI

Orange Bowl Stadium (1937), Coral Gables, Florida

No other college football stadium has hosted more memorable, exciting, and historic battles than the Orange Bowl.

Opened for play in 1937, it has hosted five Super Bowls, 11 collegiate National Championship games, and has been home to both the NFL's Miami Dolphins, as well as the University of Miami's football program.

On December 10, 1937, the Hurricanes dedicated their stadium in a game against the University of Georgia. Original seating capacity was 22,000. Renovations in 1947, '77, and '94 have boosted capacity to an impressive 74,476. The stadium also boasts an electronic scoreboard system, along with impressive press box facilities.

The University of Miami started their string of National Championships in the Orange Bowl by defeating one of the greatest college football teams of all-time, Nebraska, 31-30 capping the 1983 season. Miami then proceeded to win championships in the stadium following the '87 and '91 seasons.

Overall, the University of Miami has made the Orange Bowl the most devastating and intimidating place to play in all of college football. The Hurricanes also hold the NCAA mark for most consecutive home victories.

NICKNAME: Hurricanes
MASCOT: Sebastian
PLAYING SURFACE: Grass
SEATING CAPACITY: 74,476
CURRENT HEAD COACH: Larry Coker
NOTABLE PLAYERS/COACHES: Players: Jim Kelly, Bernie Kozar, Vinny Testaverde, Michael Irvin, Ted Hendricks, Jerome Brown, Cortez Kennedy, Russell Maryland, Gino Torretta, Warren Sapp, Jesse Armstead, Ray Lewis. **Coaches:** Andy Gustafson, Howard Schnellenberger, Jimmy Johnson, Dennis Erickson, Larry Coker.

Photo credits: JC Ridley

PITTSBURGH

Heinz Field (2001), Pittsburgh, Pennsylvania

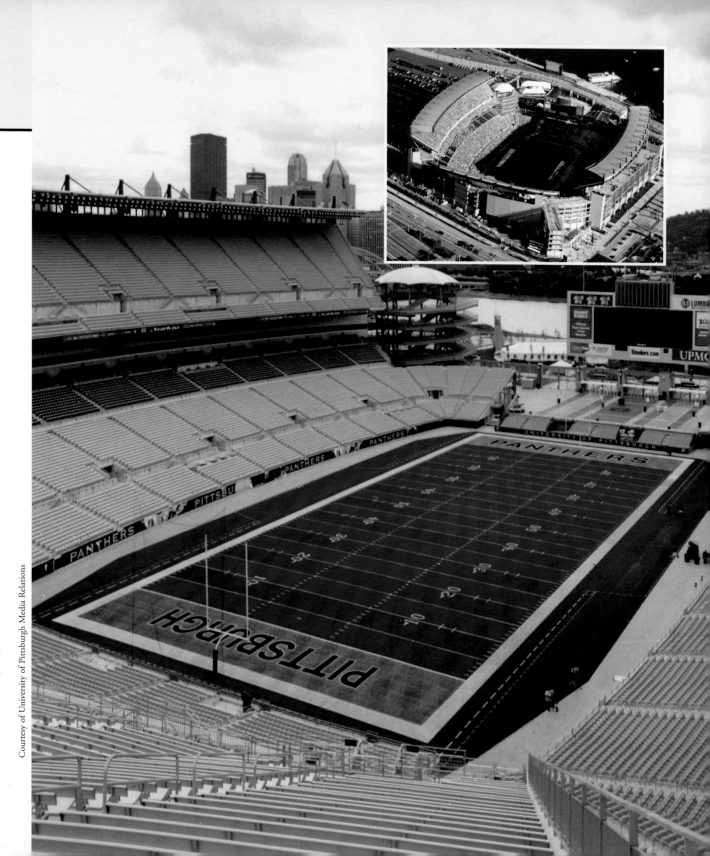

The Pitt Panthers have moved from the historic, yet outdated, Pitt Stadium, to the immaculate and brand new Heinz Field, sharing their home with the National Football League's Steelers. Since the mid-1920's, the Panthers have engraved some of college football's most indelible memories inside the legendary Pitt Stadium, where they have dominated visiting teams in route to winning a number of college football National Championships.

The Panther's new home is a magnificent football venue. The structure is shaped in the form of a horseshoe, which allows spectators unobstructed views of the field and the Pittsburgh skyline.

In comparison to their former home, Heinz Field's 65,000 seats are all chair back, versus only 132 at the old stadium. The seats are also more than forty feet closer to the field.

Pitt's current home also boasts a heated grass playing surface and the Duratz Locker Room, which is a secured area used solely by the Panthers. Upgrades include more than 400 television monitors and two video walls.

Pit Stadium will always hold a special place in every true college football fan's heart, but Heinz Field will propel Pitt football back to its rightful place atop the college football world.

NICKNAME: Panthers
MASCOT: The Panther
PLAYING SURFACE: Grass
SEATING CAPACITY: 65,000
CURRENT HEAD COACH: Walt Harris
NOTABLE PLAYERS/COACHES: **Players:** Mike Ditka, Tony Dorsett, Hugh Green, Dan Marino, Bill Fralic. **Coaches:** Jack Sutherland, Johnny Majors, Jackie Sherrill.

Courtesy of University of Pittsburgh Media Relations

RUTGERS

College football was born on the Rutgers campus November 6, 1869, as the Scarlet Knights played the Princeton Tigers. Since that day, the game we affectionately embrace has changed drastically. But the love affair, which Rutgers University has for football hasn't changed.

The Scarlet Knights play their home games in the relatively new Rutgers Stadium, which sits on the same site as the old facility. It is simply huge compared to its predecessor, which housed just 23,000-seats. Since the move, the Scarlet Knights have competed honorably against the imposing Big East Conference competition.

The stadium is home to two magnificent upper decks, a luxurious press box, many concession stands, and restroom facilities, as well as a modern day scoreboard and message center. Impressively it has already hosted the four largest crowds in the history of Rutger's football.

Fan support has always been a constant for the football program, no matter what venue they play in. The old facility consistently sold out, once packing in over 31,000 spectators for the 1988 homecoming game against Temple. With the advent of extra seating in the new venue, sellouts should be quite common.

NICKNAME: Scarlet Knights
MASCOT: The Scarlet Knight
PLAYING SURFACE: Grass
SEATING CAPACITY: 42,000
CURRENT HEAD COACH: Greg Schiano
NOTABLE PLAYERS/COACHES: Players: Leon Root, Larry Christoff, "JJ" Jennings, Bill Pickel. **Coaches:** George Foster Sanford, Harvey J. Harman, John F. Bateman, Frank R. Burns.

Photo credits: Larry Levanti/Rutgers

SYRACUSE

Carrier Dome (1980), Syracuse, New York

Opened for play in 1980, the Carrier Dome is home to the Syracuse University football team. The facility also houses one of the loudest crowds in the entire nation, which offers the Orangemen a home field advantage that few other schools can boast.

The Carrier Dome, which also is home to the Orangemen basketball team, has the capacity to seat over 50,000 frenzied spectators. Syracuse's initial home game in the Dome was against Miami of Ohio in front of 50,564 fans. Since that game the Orangemen have played at home in front of near capacity crowds many times. Syracuse also has enjoyed several undefeated home seasons in the friendly confines of the Carrier Dome.

Finished in 1980, the Dome was constructed at a cost of 28 million dollars. Besides housing a gorgeous artificial playing surface, the facility also boasts some of the nation's best stadium amenities. The Syracuse Orangemen football Hall of Fame is also housed inside the Carrier Dome, located inside the Ernie Davis Room. It is named in honor of the great Heisman Trophy running back that became the first African American to win the award following the 1961 season.

NICKNAME: Orangemen
MASCOT: Otto
PLAYING SURFACE: Artificial Turf
SEATING CAPACITY: 50,000
CURRENT HEAD COACH: Paul Pasqualoni
NOTABLE PLAYERS/COACHES: **Players:** Jim Brown, Ernie Davis, Floyd Little, Larry Csonka, Donovan McNabb. **Coaches:** Ben Schwartzwalder, Dick MacPherson, Paul Pasqualoni.

TEMPLE

Veterans Stadium (1971), Philadelphia, Pennsylvania

Temple fans be prepared. Your team is on the rise. Head coach Bobby Wallace had the Owls playing exciting and confident football last year and this upcoming season promises an even better product.

Much like the University of Miami did for many years, Temple shares their home field with an NFL team. Veterans Stadium is home to the Owls and boasts an impressive capacity 66,592. Temple will undoubtedly increase their average home attendance this year, which is in direct correlation with the type of up-and-coming football squad they will field.

The "Vet" has long been regarded as one of the toughest stadiums to come to by both opposing NFL and collegiate football teams due to the loud and raucous noise displayed by the knowledgeable Philadelphia football fans.

Though Veterans Stadium has hosted its share of great football games, relatively few have been of the college variety. That trend will no doubt change in the near future because, like the Philadelphia Eagles, the Temple Owls seem primed to become a contender themselves. One thing is certain concerning Veterans Stadium; once an opposing team visits the unfriendly confines, they better be prepared to meet the wrath of Philly fans.

NICKNAME: Owls
MASCOT: The Owl
PLAYING SURFACE: Artificial Turf
SEATING CAPACITY: 66,592
CURRENT HEAD COACH: Bobby Wallace
NOTABLE PLAYERS/COACHES: **Players:** Steve Joachim, Tre Johnson, Stacey Mack, Paul Palmer, Larry Chester. **Coaches:** Glenn "Pop" Warner, Wayne Hardin.

VIRGINIA TECH

Lane Stadium/Worsham Field (1965), Blacksburg, Virginia

Virginia Tech football has skyrocketed over the past ten years. The Hokies consistently play in big bowl games and annually threaten to win the National Championship. Head Coach Frank Beamer and the entire Hokie nation have catapulted to the very top level of college football.

Much like the rise of the Hokie program, has been the elevation in comfort and beauty of Lane Stadium/Worsham Field. Virginia Tech opened the stadium in 1965 with a win over William and Mary, 9-7. Currently Worsham Field is one of the most intimidating places to play for opposing teams.

The stadium originally seated 40,000 fans, but presently seats over 51,600. Currently, Lane Stadium is undergoing yet another renovation, which will increase seating capacity to accommodate up to 15,000 more fans.

The first nationally televised game in the stadium took place on Thanksgiving Day 1982, against archrival Virginia. Tech won 21-14 under their newly constructed lights.

The stadium is named after Edward H. Lane who was a graduate of Virginia Tech, and helped donate and raise a great deal of money for the University. The field is named in honor of Wes and Janet Worsham who also contributed generously to the betterment of Virginia Tech.

NICKNAME: Hokies
MASCOT: The Hokie Bird
PLAYING SURFACE: Natural Grass
SEATING CAPACITY: 51,620
CURRENT HEAD COACH: Frank Beamer
NOTABLE PLAYERS/COACHES: **Players:** Bruce Smith, Carroll Dale, Michael Vick. **Coaches:** Jerry Claiborne, Bill Dooley, Frank Beamer.

Photographs courtesy of Virginia Tech Sports Information

Photo credit: Mike Hardy

WEST VIRGINIA

Mountaineer Field (1980), Morgantown, West Virginia

Beautiful Mountaineer Field is home to the West Virginia football team and has one of the nation's best overall sporting facilities.

Built in 1980, Mountaineer Field had an original capacity of 50,000-seats, but after renovations, seating increased to 63,500. Complete with an electronic scoreboard system, luxury suites, modern lighting system, and a spacious press box, Mountaineer Field is an impressive place to watch a college football game.

West Virginia fans are loud, knowledgeable, and have always supported their beloved Mountaineer teams. Crowds close to 70,000, have packed Mountaineer Field to watch great Big East Conference football.

Head Coach Rich Rodriguez and the hometown crowd will undoubtedly keep the Mountaineer football program at or near the top of the Big East Conference.

NICKNAME: Mountaineers
MASCOT: The Mountaineer
PLAYING SURFACE: Artificial Turf
SEATING CAPACITY: 63,500
CURRENT HEAD COACH: Rich Rodriguez
NOTABLE PLAYERS/COACHES: Players: Jeff Hostetler, Major Harris, Aaron Beasley, James Jett, Amos Zereoue. **Coaches:** Bobby Bowden, Don Nehlen.

ILLINOIS

INDIANA

IOWA

MICHIGAN

MICHIGAN STATE

MINNESOTA

NORTHWESTERN

OHIO STATE

PENN STATE

PURDUE

WISCONSIN

THE BIG TEN CONFERENCE

Few college football conferences past or present can boast teams, which play such a fierce and hard-nosed brand of football. In much the same way few leagues are home to such mammoth and picturesque stadiums. Three of the four biggest on-campus facilities reside within the Big Ten, the largest being "The Big House", which is home to the University of Michigan.

Of course, the stadiums aren't the only reasons why the Big Ten is so popular. There are and have been, as you might have guessed, tremendous players and teams. The Big Ten is home to numerous Heisman Trophy winners, National Championship teams, as well as legendary coaches. But this book is centered on the stadiums by which these greats could apply their trade.

Annually, the Big Ten teams lead the nation in conference average attendance, which is undoubtedly related to the type of football played. The loyalty and love of football shown by fans associated with the Big Ten is not all together unique, but the number of people, who attend these facilities each year, are.

ILLINOIS

Memorial Stadium (1924), Urbana-Champaign, Illinois

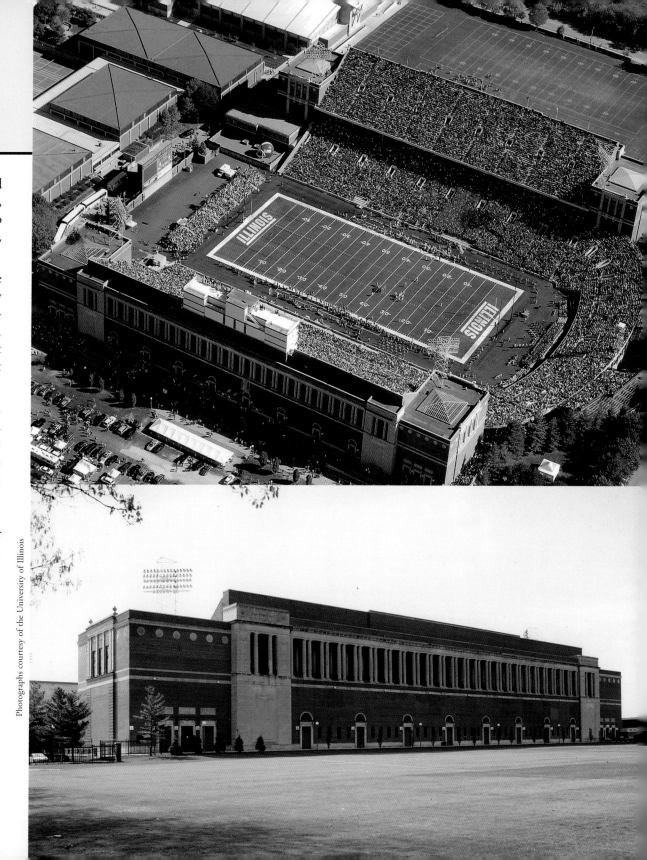

Memorial Stadium/Zuppke Field is a gorgeous mixture of traditional and contemporary architecture and design. The legendary Memorial Stadium, built in 1923, was named in honor of the University of Illinois students who gave their lives in World War I. The field is named for Robert C. Zuppke, the outstanding head coach, who led the Illini from 1913 - 1941.

Though Memorial Stadium opened for play on November 3, 1923 as the Fighting Illini defeated Chicago 7-0, the most memorable day in its history was to take place the next season. On October 18, 1924, the day it was officially dedicated, the University of Illinois defeated rival Michigan 39-14, behind the legendary performance of halfback Harold "Red" Grange. That day, Grange accounted for six touchdowns in leading the Illini to its biggest victory in school history.

This gorgeous facility enjoys all the amenities that a top-flight program should have. Memorial Stadium is home to many luxury box suites and a modern press box area. Next to the overall design and architecture, the two most impressive attributes are the contemporary scoreboard and Grange Rock. Installed for the 1994 season, the scoreboard offers fans and players all they could want in an entertainment system, while "Red" Grange Rock, which sits at the north end zone, was dedicated October 22, 1994.

Attendance figures of well over 70,000 have been recorded on a number of occasions. One of the largest took place in 1984, as 78,297 watched Illinois play Missouri.

NICKNAME: Fighting Illini
MASCOT: No Mascot
PLAYING SURFACE: Grass
SEATING CAPACITY: 70,900
CURRENT HEAD COACH: Ron Turner
NOTABLE PLAYERS/COACHES: **Players:** George Halas, Red Grange, Buddy Young, Ray Nitschke, Bill Burrell, Ed O'Bradovich, Dick Butkus, Tony Eason, Dana Howard, Kevin Hardy. **Coaches:** Edgar G. Holt, Robert C. Zuppke, John Mackovic, Ron Turner.

Photographs courtesy of the University of Illinois

Top: ©IU Athletics Photography/Paul Riley

Photo credit:Getty Images North America

INDIANA

Memorial Stadium (1960), Bloomington, Indiana

Memorial Stadium is home to the Hoosier Football Team. Built in 1960, Memorial Stadium originally housed wooden seats until aluminum boards were installed before the 1985 season. "The House" as it is commonly referred to by Hoosier faithful, is one of the Big Ten's toughest venues to play in for visiting teams. From 1987 through the 1994 season Indiana boasted an impressive 31-9-1 record.

Since its inaugural season, "The House" has undergone a number of renovations, which make it a great setting for college football. Indiana added a new state-of-the-art lighting system before the 1988 season, brand new computerized scoreboards at both ends of the stadium in 1989, and an updated press box. Although artificial turf was added in 1986, Indiana has since gone back to playing on natural grass.

Head coach Gerry Dinardo hopes the wild and raucous Indiana crowds will help the Hoosiers secure victory upon victory in Memorial Stadium.

NICKNAME: Hoosiers
MASCOT: No Mascot
PLAYING SURFACE: Natural Grass
SEATING CAPACITY: 52,354
CURRENT HEAD COACH: Gerry Dinardo
NOTABLE PLAYERS/COACHES: **Players:** Trent Green, Dan Stryzinski, Anthony Thompson, Alex Smith, Antwaan Randle El. **Coaches:** Lee Corso, Bill Mallory.

IOWA

Kinnick Stadium (1929), Iowa City, Iowa

In 1939, Iowa superstar Nile Kinnick won the Heisman Trophy and the hearts of many adoring fans throughout the Midwest. Formerly Iowa Stadium, it became Kinnick Stadium in1972 in honor of the noted player.

Built in 1929, the stadium, like most facilities around the nation, has since undergone a number of renovations. In 1956, due to the addition of end zone seats, capacity was raised to 60,000. By 1983, stadium capacity was again enlarged to 66,000-seats, and currently sits at 70,397.

Not only has capacity risen in historic Kinnick Stadium, the addition of a multi-million dollar press box, along with the institution of a gorgeous scoreboard system, have made this facility the envy of many programs.

Though the Hawkeyes played a number of seasons on artificial turf, natural grass was reinstated prior to the 1989 season.

The Hawkeyes have enjoyed much success within the friendly confines of Kinnick Stadium; going undefeated at home a number of different times.

NICKNAME: Hawkeyes
MASCOT: Herky
PLAYING SURFACE: Natural Grass
SEATING CAPACITY: 70,397
CURRENT HEAD COACH: Kirk Ferentz
NOTABLE PLAYERS/COACHES: **Players:** Ozzie Simmons, Nile Kinnick, Chuck Long. **Coaches:** Howard Jones, Forest Evashevski, Hayden Fry.

Photographs courtesy of the University of Iowa

Photo credit: Danny Moloshok/Allsport

Top: ©U-M Photo Services

MICHIGAN

Michigan Stadium (1927), Ann Arbor, Michigan

Michigan Stadium, the nation's largest on-campus venue, commonly known as "The Big House", is a marvel of architectural genius. It was constructed in the late 1920's upon the urging of coaching-great Fielding Yost, who felt that the University of Michigan could easily draw well over 100,000 spectators to every home game.

The Wolverines originally played their home games at Regents Field, where they amassed an incredible 87-2-3 record. From there, the team moved to Ferry Field in 1902. Ferry's largest capacity was 40,000. Soon after the move, Coach Yost was lobbying for a new stadium.

The land purchased for the construction of the new stadium was home to an underground spring. Because of the water content and unstable area, it was determined the land had to be lowered so construction could take place. One of the cranes used for the project sunk during construction, and remains beneath the stadium to this day.

The new stadium opened, with 84,401 seats, on October 1, 1927, with the Wolverines defeating Ohio Wesleyan 33-0. In 1930, it became the first facility to use electronic scoreboards for official time use. It has undergone many seating changes through the years. By 1973, Michigan Stadium had surpassed the 100,000-seat plateau.

On November 8, 1975, the Wolverines hosted Purdue in front of 102,415 spectators. This game started a consecutive streak in which Michigan has played in front at least 100,000 fans in every home game.

NICKNAME: Wolverines
MASCOT: No Mascot
PLAYING SURFACE: Natural Grass
SEATING CAPACITY: 107,501
CURRENT HEAD COACH: Lloyd Carr
NOTABLE PLAYERS/COACHES: Players: Tom Harmon, former U.S. President Gerald Ford, Desmond Howard, and Charles Woodson. **Coaches:** Fielding "Hurry Up" Yost, Glenn "Bo" Schembechler, Lloyd Carr.

Autumn's Cathedrals   25

MICHIGAN STATE

Spartan Stadium (1923), East Lansing, Michigan

Spartan Stadium is where the Michigan State football team calls home. Originally built in 1923, Spartan Stadium boasts an impressive seating capacity of 72,027. When built, capacity was just 14,000-seats, but the stadium underwent major seating renovations in 1935, '48, '56, and '57.

The Spartans played on a beautiful artificial turf surface for many years. They played their first game on artificial turf in 1969, though the actual surface has been changed for player safety a number of times. The surface was changed once again in 2002 to grass.

Through the years, Michigan State teams have consistently challenged conference foes for the Big Ten's top spot. Their success is partially due; in no small part, to the loyal Spartan fans. On a number of occasions, crowds surpassing 80,000 have packed the stadium to watch Big Ten football.

Spartan Stadium has been home to a couple of National Championship teams, numerous great MSU players, as well as some great coaches in its storied history.

NICKNAME: Spartans
MASCOT: Sparty
PLAYING SURFACE: Grass
SEATING CAPACITY: 72,027
CURRENT HEAD COACH: Bobby Williams
NOTABLE PLAYERS/COACHES: **Players:** Bubba Smith, Kirk Gibson, Tony Mandrich, Andre Rison, T.J. Duckett. **Coaches:** Clarence "Biggie" Munn, Duffy Daugherty, George Perles.

Top: Courtesy Michigan State

Photo credit: Associated Press, AP

MINNESOTA

Hubert H. Humphrey Metrodome (1982), Minneapolis, Minnesota

Before the University of Minnesota Golden Gophers moved into the comfortable Hubert H. Humphrey Metrodome in 1982, they played their football games in frigid Memorial Stadium, from 1924-1981.

The first thirty-five years inside Memorial Stadium, the Golden Gophers played in a venue which had a seating capacity of only 52,809. Seating was raised to 56,652 in the stadium for the Golden Gopher's final eleven years. By 1982, U of M had made their new home the state-of-the-art Metrodome, which had an original capacity for Gopher games of 62,218. The largest crowd to witness a Golden Gopher home football game inside the Metrodome took place November 1986, when Minnesota played Iowa in front of 65,018 rabid fans.

Due to the arctic climate in Minnesota, the move from Memorial Stadium to the luxurious Metrodome was only logical. Inside the Dome are such amenities as air-controlled climate, comfortable seating for all, as well as an enthusiastic home crowd.

Current head football coach Glen Mason has excelled in bringing back a hard-nosed style of football, which is reminiscent of Gopher glory years of past.

NICKNAME: Golden Gophers
MASCOT: Goldy
PLAYING SURFACE: Artificial Turf
SEATING CAPACITY: 64,172
CURRENT HEAD COACH: Glen Mason
NOTABLE PLAYERS/COACHES: Players: Bronko Nagurski, Leo Nomellini, Bobby Bell, Tyrone Carter. **Coaches:** Bernie Biernman, Murray Warmath, Lou Holtz.

NORTHWESTERN

Dyche Stadium/Ryan Field (1942), Evanston, Illinois

Dyche Stadium/Ryan Field, which sits snuggly on the Northwestern campus, has been a fixture for the University since its opening in 1926.

Dyche Stadium is named in honor of the former university Vice-President, William A. Dyche. Over the past eight seasons, the Wildcat football program has been elevated to top status within the Big-10 Conference. The facility has rapidly emerged as the place to be for Northwestern fans on Saturday afternoons in autumn. Original seating capacity for the stadium was 45,000-seats, but was quickly enlarged to accommodate over 49,000 spectators by the 1949 season. Throughout the 1940's and 50's, the Wildcats averaged over 40,000 per home game in Dyche's stadium. The Wildcats best season for home attendance was 1960, averaging 50,600 spectators.

As the years rolled by, Dyche Stadium/Ryan Field has undergone many upgrades to its facilities. Not only has the stadium been modernized to keep up with the rest of the Big-10 facilities, it has also hosted some of the most exciting collegiate football games in modern history.

NICKNAME: Wildcats
MASCOT: Willy
PLAYING SURFACE: Grass
SEATING CAPACITY: 47,130
CURRENT HEAD COACH: Randy Walker
NOTABLE PLAYERS/COACHES: **Players:** Moon Baker, Otto Graham, Ron Burton, Darnell Autry, Zak Kustok, Damien Anderson. **Coaches:** Bob Voigts, Ara Parseghian, Gary Barnett, Randy Walker.

Top: Getty Images North America

Courtesy of Media Services Northwestern Athletics

THE OHIO STATE

Ohio Stadium (1922), Columbus, Ohio

Few places in college football are as noticeable or recognizable as Ohio Stadium. It is affectionately known as, "The Horseshoe". Since its beginning in 1922, Ohio Stadium has stood as one of college footballs most enduring landmarks and greatest attractions.

The Buckeyes opened the stadium in October 1922, against Ohio Wesleyan. Although original capacity in "The Horseshoe" was 66,210, 71,385 fans crammed the new facility two weeks later as the Buckeyes hosted Michigan on dedication day.

As with all long-standing sporting venues, Ohio Stadium has also undergone a number of renovations to seating, as well as to its playing surface. During the first forty-nine seasons, the Ohio State football team played on natural grass. Then beginning in 1971 and ending after the 1989 season, artificial turf was the playing surface of choice. Since the start of the 1990 season, Ohio Stadium boasts one of the nation's prettiest and durable Prescription Athletic Turf fields.

To keep in line with a number of other Big Ten schools, which incorporate the services of scoreboard electronic systems, Ohio Stadium added their own modernized scoreboard system.

Few college football stadiums offer the types of views as Ohio Stadium, which is nestled beautifully next to the Olentangy River.

NICKNAME: Buckeyes
MASCOT: Brutus
PLAYING SURFACE: Prescription Playing Turf (Grass)
SEATING CAPACITY: 101,568
CURRENT HEAD COACH: Jim Tressel
NOTABLE PLAYERS/COACHES: Players: Les Horvath, Vic Janowicz, Howard Cassady, Archie Griffin, Eddie George. With all do respect to The Ohio State University, there are just too many more great players to list. **Coaches:** Paul Brown, Wes Fesler, Woody Hayes.

PENN STATE

Beaver Stadium (1960), State College, Pennsylvania

Beaver Stadium, home to Penn State football is set in peaceful Happy Valley. Before being stationed at its current location in 1960, the stadium was known as Beaver Field, a 30,000-seat venue, which was located approximately one mile west of where the facility now resides. Beaver Field was the home of the Nittany Lion football program from 1909 through the 1959 season.

The stadium, named in honor of Civil War veteran and former Pennsylvania Governor James A. Beaver, was dedicated September 17, 1960 as Penn hosted Boston College.

Capacity at Beaver Stadium is over 106,000-seats, which makes it the second largest on-campus facility in the nation, second only to the University of Michigan.

The addition of Penn State University to the Big Ten in the early 1990's, has elevated an already proud and tradition rich conference to another level.

NICKNAME: Nittany Lions
MASCOT: The Nittany Lion
PLAYING SURFACE: Natural Grass
SEATING CAPACITY: 106,500
CURRENT HEAD COACH: Joe Paterno
NOTABLE PLAYERS/COACHES: **Players:** Jack Hamm, Franco Harris, John Cappelletti, Matt Millen, Todd Blackledge, Kerry Collins. **Coaches:** Bob Higgins, Charles "Rip" Engle, Joe Paterno.

Courtesy of Penn State University

Courtesy of Purdue University

PURDUE

Ross-Ade Stadium (1924), West Lafayette, Indiana

Much like the other magnificent Big Ten football venues, Ross-Ade Stadium is full of beautiful and breath-taking scenery.

Built in 1924, Ross-Ade's original capacity was just 13,500-seats. The stadium has undergone a number of upgrades, which would eventually bring the facility to its current capacity of 67,861.

Purdue teams have played in front of home sellout crowds often, doing so 17 consecutive times, starting in 1979 and ending in 1981. In fact, Purdue has managed to play in front of home crowds exceeding 70,000 fans many times.

The home of the Boilermakers took its name in honor of two men, David E. Ross and George Ade, who purchased a sixty-five acre patch of land on which the stadium now sits.

Because of the generosity of both Mr. Ross and Mr. Ade, the Big Ten faithful have been treated to fun and exciting football in this fan friendly facility over the past 77 seasons.

One side note concerning Ross-Ade Stadium is that, unlike the other Big Ten Conference facilities, Purdue has never been home to an artificial turf surface.

NICKNAME:	Boilermakers
MASCOT:	Purdue Pete
PLAYING SURFACE:	Natural Grass
SEATING CAPACITY:	67,861
CURRENT HEAD COACH:	Joe Tiller

NOTABLE PLAYERS/COACHES: Players: Bob Griese, Leroy Keyes, Rod Woodson, Mike Alstott, Drew Brees. **Coaches:** Jack Mollenkopf, Jim Young, Joe Tiller.

WISCONSIN

Camp Randall Stadium (1917), Madison, Wisconsin

Camp Randall, which was re-constructed in 1917, is a massive structure built in the shape of a horseshoe. The land where Camp Randall Stadium is presently erected was also the home for the original stadium, which was built in 1913.

Original capacity in the stadium was 10,000-seats in 1917. Changes in 1994 actually lowered the seating total from 77,745 to 76,129, which is where it stands today.

Every facility has its own distinctive history, especially concerning construction, and the story behind Camp Randall is no different. Historically speaking, the area, which is home to the stadium, may be as important to the United States as any college football facility in the nation. It was a former military installation home to a military training center during the Civil War, in which an estimated 70,000 troops passed through.

NICKNAME: Badgers
MASCOT: Bucky
PLAYING SURFACE: Artificial Turf
SEATING CAPACITY: 76,129
CURRENT HEAD COACH: Barry Alvarez
NOTABLE PLAYERS/COACHES: **Players:** Alan Ameche, Jerry Wunsch, Troy Vincent, Cory Raymer, Aaron Gibson, Ron Dayne, Chris Chambers, Michael Bennett. **Coaches:** Milt Bruhn, Dave McClain, Barry Alvarez.

Courtesy of Wisconsin Sports Information

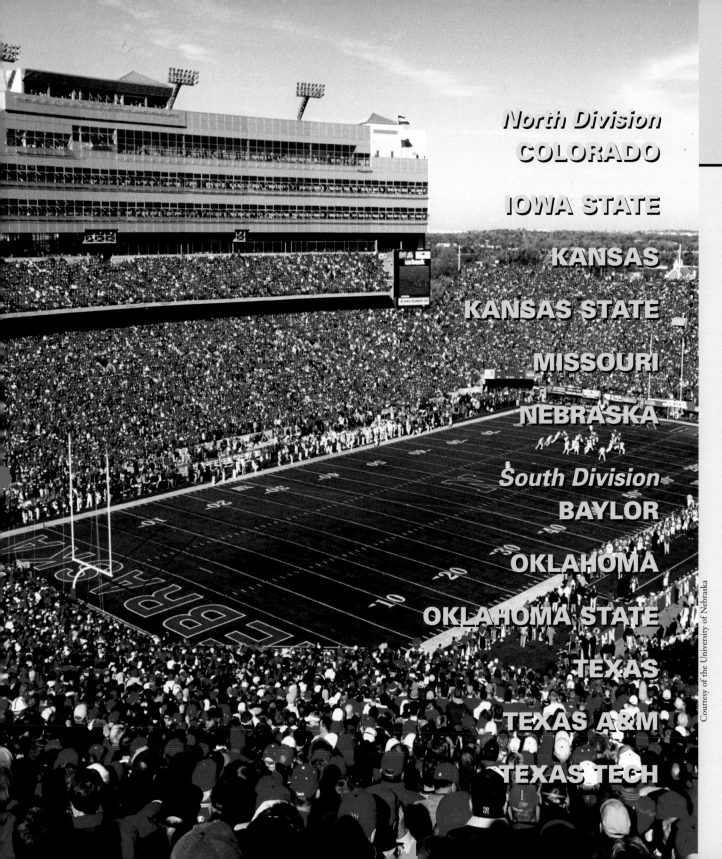

North Division
COLORADO

IOWA STATE

KANSAS

KANSAS STATE

MISSOURI

NEBRASKA

South Division
BAYLOR

OKLAHOMA

OKLAHOMA STATE

TEXAS

TEXAS A&M

TEXAS TECH

Courtesy of the University of Nebraska

THE BIG TWELVE CONFERENCE

The Big 12 is a creation of the old Big 8 Conference mixed with four of the previous members of the now extinct Southwest Conference.

Powerhouses, such as Oklahoma, Nebraska, Texas, and Texas A&M, bring unlimited tradition to the Big 12, while recent powers like Bill Snyder's Kansas State Wildcats and Gary Barnett's Colorado Buffaloes can play with and beat the best teams on any given Saturday. Iowa State, Missouri, Texas Tech, Baylor, Kansas, and Oklahoma State all have programs, which are well on their way to being consistently ranked with the nation's top twenty-five teams.

The Stadiums and crowds, which the teams of the Big 12 play in and in front of, are mirror images of each other. For example, the fans at Texas A&M's Kyle Field are extremely loud, very knowledgeable, and generally hard-nosed, just like R.C. Slocum's Aggie football teams. This is also the case in Norman, Oklahoma, where Sooner fans are tough yet classy, like the coaches and players of the OU football program.

The stadiums, which house these teams are as scenic, monumental, and awe-inspiring as any in the nation.

COLORADO

Folsom Field (1924), Boulder, Colorado

Folsom Field sits quaintly on the campus of the University of Colorado in scenic Boulder. Set against the Front Range of the Rocky Mountains, it showcases an exciting football team along with loyal Buff fans.

Folsom Field is named for former CU Head Football Coach Frederick Folsom. Opening day, November 1, 1924, the Buffs blew-out Regis College 31-0. The stadium's original name was Colorado Stadium but was renamed Folsom Field after Folsom's death in 1944.

The stadium is simply gorgeous, boasting awe-inspiring architecture. It comes complete with comfortable aluminum seating, a huge and luxurious six-level press box that towers over the western grandstands, a gorgeous natural grass playing surface, along with the magnificent Dal Ward Center, which sits just beyond the north end zone. The Dallas Ward Center is a 92,000-foot athletic facility, which houses a monstrous weight room, sports medicine, kitchen, and dining areas.

Fan support is as impressive as the stadium itself. Throughout Folsom Field's existence, the Buffs have played before sell-out crowds many times. It seems that every time Oklahoma or Nebraska come to town, a new attendance record is set.

There may not be another facility anywhere, which offers spectators such gorgeous scenery.

NICKNAME: Buffaloes
MASCOT: Ralphie & Chip
PLAYING SURFACE: Natural Grass
SEATING CAPACITY: 51,748
CURRENT HEAD COACH: Gary Barnett
NOTABLE PLAYERS/COACHES: Players: Byron "Whizzer" White, Dick Anderson, Eric Bienemy, Rashaan Salaam. **Coaches:** Frederick Folsom, Dallas Ward, Bill McCartney.

Photo credit: Gary Clarke Photographs

IOWA STATE

Jack Trice Stadium (1975), Ames, Iowa

Jack Trice Stadium is home to a talented team, which is on the rise in the Big 12 Conference. It houses a modest seating-capacity, with first-rate amenities, which include; luxury units and a state-of-the-art scoreboard.

The facility was known as Cyclone Stadium until 1977, when it was renamed Jack Trice Stadium, in honor of the first African-American athlete to play at Iowa State.

In 1975, Jack Trice Stadium opened to an impressive average home attendance of 39,774. Since that initial season, fans have continued to support the team, averaging over 50,000 per game for an entire season several times. One of the great and memorable games in Iowa State history took place in 1990 as 54,475 spectators packed the stadium to watch Iowa State upset Nebraska.

With the addition of the four schools from the old Southwest Conference, Iowa State fans can now see traditional powers such Texas and Texas A&M, along with their long standing rivals Oklahoma and Nebraska.

NICKNAME:	Cyclones
MASCOT:	Cy
PLAYING SURFACE:	Natural Grass
SEATING CAPACITY:	43,000
CURRENT HEAD COACH:	Dan McCarney

NOTABLE PLAYERS/COACHES: Players: Marcus Robertson, Troy Davis, James Reed. **Coaches:** Johnny Majors, Earle Bruce, Dan McCarney.

KANSAS

Kansas Memorial Stadium (1921), Lawrence, Kansas

Kansas Memorial Stadium, built on the grounds where McCook Field (Kansas' original football field) used to sit, is one of the oldest college football stadiums in the nation. It is the first structure built on a college campus west of the Mississippi River.

Opened for play in 1921, Kansas won its first game at Memorial Stadium against rival Kansas State University 21-7 before 5,160 fans. Original capacity was 22,000 seats.

Hall of Fame basketball coach "Phog" Allen was the football coach for the Jayhawks during the 1920 season, and was very influential in the drive to build a new facility. After a 20-0 comeback against Nebraska, which ultimately ended in a 20-20 tie that season, many fans gathered for a rally the following Monday to celebrate the game's outcome, and to raise money for a new modern facility. During the rally, more than $200,000 was pledged towards the new new stadium, which was ultimately built in time for the 1921 season.

Artificial turf, which first supplanted natural grass in 1970, has been replaced twice, most recently prior to the 1990 season.

NICKNAME: Jayhawks
MASCOT: Big J
PLAYING SURFACE: Artificial Turf
SEATING CAPACITY: 50,250
CURRENT HEAD COACH: Mark Mangino
NOTABLE PLAYERS/COACHES: Players: Gayle Sayers, John Riggins, Dana Stubblefield, Gilbert Brown. **Coaches:** Phog Allen, Pepper Rodgers, Glenn Mason.

Photo credits: Thad Alton

Photo credit: Elsa Hasch/Allsport

Top: Associated Press, AP

KANSAS STATE

KSU Stadium/Wagner Field (1968), Manhattan, Kansas

The Kansas State Wildcats play their home football games in raucous KSU Stadium/Wagner Field. Before Head Coach Bill Snyder came to Manhattan, Kansas, home field advantage was a non-factor for the Wildcats, but since 1990, Kansas State has been all but unbeatable at home.

Original capacity was 35,000 when KSU Stadium opened for play September 1968, with the Wildcats defeating Colorado State 21-0. The field is named in honor of Kansas' residents Dave and Carol Wagner.

The entire football complex has undergone a number of facelifts, which include, the introduction of artificial turf in 1970, the construction of state-of-the-art locker room facilities in 1972, and the implementation of a lighting system in 1983. Skyboxes and an indoor facility were added in 1993, making the complex one of the best in the Big 12.

Because of the winning ways enjoyed by the Kansas State football team over the past decade, fans have flocked to KSU Stadium in great numbers, selling out the facility practically every Saturday. Crowds surpassing 40,000 in attendance are the norm in Manhattan.

NICKNAME: Wildcats
MASCOT: Willy
PLAYING SURFACE: Artificial Turf
SEATING CAPACITY: 50,000
CURRENT HEAD COACH: Bill Snyder
NOTABLE PLAYERS/COACHES: Players: Steve Grogan, Michael Bishop, Martin Gramatica, Quincy Morgan. **Coaches:** Jim Dickey, Bill Snyder.

MISSOURI

Memorial Stadium/Faurot Field (1926), Columbia, Missouri

Built in 1926 and named in honor of legendary football coach and athletic director, Don Faurot, Memorial Stadium has proved to be an incredibly tough place to play for opposing teams. Boasting a capacity of over 68,000, the Missouri football team has often drawn home crowds surpassing 70,000.

Memorial Stadium, built in the shape of a bowl, is home to an impressive landmark. On the north side of the stadium sits a massive "M". Built in 1927, the "M" was constructed by the freshman class, making it 95 feet high and 90 feet wide.

For a ten-season period, from 1985 to 1994, the Missouri football team played on artificial turf. Since 1995, the new field, which is made up of Kentucky bluegrass, is one of the nicest playing surfaces in the entire nation.

The stadium has hosted a number of memorable games and players in its long and storied history, including the infamous "fifth-down" game in 1990 against Colorado, and the "miraculous-catch" game against the University of Nebraska in 1997. Though the Missouri faithful has suffered through some heart-wrenching games on Faurot Field, one thing will never change; the Tigers will always play hard against anybody who comes into their home.

NICKNAME: Tigers
MASCOT: Truman
PLAYING SURFACE: Grass
SEATING CAPACITY: 68,174
CURRENT HEAD COACH: Gary Pinkel
NOTABLE PLAYERS/COACHES: **Players:** Kellen Winslow, Otis Smith, Justin Smith. **Coaches:** Don Faurot, Dan Devine, Warren Powers.

Photo credit: Getty Images North America

Courtesy of the University of Nebraska

NEBRASKA

Memorial Stadium/Tom Osborne Field (1923)
Lincoln, Nebraska

The University of Nebraska's Memorial Stadium/Tom Osborne Field, offering one the best home field advantages in all of college football, has not hosted anything less than a sellout crowd since former coach Bob Devaney's first game in Lincoln. This streak of consecutive sellouts is the longest in the nation, showing no signs of ending in the near future.

No stadium in the nation is home to a better weight lifting facility, press box, luxury box suites, or scoreboard system.

Memorial Stadium opened its gates in front of a capacity crowd of 31,000, October 23, 1923. They battled Kansas to a scoreless tie. Though many venues carry the name Memorial Stadium, Nebraska's facility is named in honor of all the Nebraska soldiers who fought and died in every war spanning the Civil War through the Vietnam Conflict. In all four corners of the stadium one can read quotes dedicated to those warriors.

Throughout its 77 years of use, Memorial Stadium has withstood renovations and additions. Artificial turf was initially installed in 1970, but was replaced in '77 and '92. Recently the school laid down a hybrid grass-turf field.

NICKNAME: Cornhuskers
MASCOT: Herbie & Lil' Red
PLAYING SURFACE: Hybrid Turf
SEATING CAPACITY: 74,031
CURRENT HEAD COACH: Frank Solich
NOTABLE PLAYERS/COACHES: Players: Johnny Rodgers, Dave Rimington, Mike Rozier, Tommy Frazier, Eric Crouch. **Coaches:** Bob Devaney, Tom Osborne, Frank Solich.

BAYLOR

Floyd Casey Stadium (1950), Waco, Texas

Floyd Casey Stadium is one of the Big 12 Conference's nicest, all-around facilities. It took the name of the father of Carl Casey, who, along with his wife Thelma, donated over five million dollars for a major renovation project.

Built in 1950, the stadium is home to a gorgeous grass field, a beautiful letterman's lounge, a brand new press box and luxury suites, and a relatively new lighting system. The stadium also houses the immaculate Carl and Thelma Casey Athletic Center.

The first game played at the facility, which was then called Baylor Stadium, took place September 30, 1950, as the Bears defeated the University of Houston 34-7. Since that game, the Bears have registered over 140 home wins inside their friendly confines.

Before moving to their current home in 1950, the Bears enjoyed great success at other sites as well. Baylor teams won 63% of their games at Carroll Field from 1902-'25 and 1930-'35. Then, in four seasons, at the Cotton Palace (1926-'29), the Bears won 68% of the games before moving on to Municipal Stadium from 1936-'49. At Municipal Stadium, "the good guys" won close to 69% of their home games.

No matter where Baylor has called home, they have consistently dominated their opponents. Casey Stadium and the entire Baylor program are working hard to regain dominance in arguably the nation's toughest conference.

NICKNAME: Bears
MASCOT: Joy
PLAYING SURFACE: Grass
SEATING CAPACITY: 50,000
CURRENT HEAD COACH: Kevin Steele
NOTABLE PLAYERS/COACHES: **Players:** Barton Koch, Jim Ray Smith, Mike Singletary. **Coaches:** John Bridgers, Grant Teaff.

Photo credit: Ronald Martinez/Allsport

Top: Courtesy of the University of Oklahoma

OKLAHOMA

Oklahoma Memorial Stadium/Owen Field (1925)
Norman, Oklahoma

Winner of seven National Championships, the Oklahoma Sooners are back where college football needs them—at the top.

Memorial Stadium/Owen Field is home to one of college football's most enduring programs. From Coach Wilkinson and the famous 47-game winning streak, to Coach Switzer and his band of hardnose rebels, to the current edition of Sooner-football with Coach Stoops at the controls, Memorial Stadium has hosted it all. The field is named for the great Beanie Owen, who coached the Sooners from 1905-1926.

With the exception of a few years in the 1990's, when Oklahoma wasn't "Oklahoma", the Sooners often ran up 50 plus points against any and all opponents at home.

Stadium amenities include; a top-of-the-line lighting system, 75,762 seats, a gorgeous field with an outstanding drainage system, and comfortable seating for the very vociferous and electric Sooner fans.

Memorial Stadium/Owen Field is undergoing a major renovation and facelift as this book goes to press.

NICKNAME: Sooners
MASCOT: Sooner Schooner
PLAYING SURFACE: Grass
SEATING CAPACITY: 75,762
CURRENT HEAD COACH: Bob Stoops
NOTABLE PLAYERS/COACHES: **Players:** Billy Vessels, Jim Owens, Steve Owens, Jack Mildren, The Selmon Brothers, Billy Simms, Keith Jackson, Brian Bosworth and too many other Sooner superstars to mention. **Coaches:** Bud Wilkinson, Barry Switzer, Bob Stoops.

Autumn's Cathedrals   41

OKLAHOMA STATE

Lewis Field (1920), Stillwater, Oklahoma

Lewis Stadium is the long time home for the Oklahoma State Cowboys. Named for a popular and beloved former dean of veterinary medicine, Laymon Lowery Lewis, the field actually opened for play in 1913.

Lewis Field became Lewis Stadium in 1920 due to the addition of 8,000 grandstand seats. What makes it unique in nature is the fact that the stadium had to be re-constructed to an east-west configuration to nullify the strong winds of Stillwater, Oklahoma.

Over the years the facility has undergone a number of renovations, which have made it one of the nicest and most comfortable facilities in the Big 12. Some of the state-of-the-art amenities, which were added through the years include; the coaches building in 1978, a multi-million dollar press box in 1980, and a permanent lighting system in 1985.

NICKNAME:	Cowboys
MASCOT:	Pistol Pete
PLAYING SURFACE:	Artificial Turf
SEATING CAPACITY:	50,614
CURRENT HEAD COACH:	Les Miles

NOTABLE PLAYERS/COACHES: Players: Terry Miller, Thurman Thomas, Barry Sanders. **Coaches:** Jim Lookabaugh, Jimmy Johnson, Pat Jones.

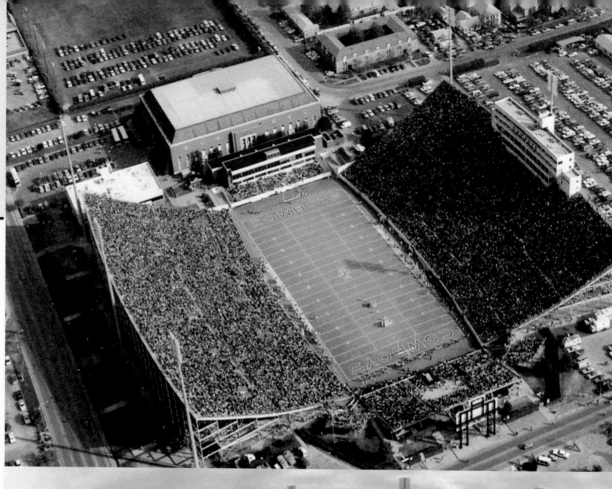

Photo credit: Associated Press, AP   Top: Courtesy of Oklahoma State

TEXAS

Darrell K. Royal-Memorial Stadium (1924)
Austin, Texas

Opening in 1924, Darrell K. Royal-Memorial Stadium is a beautifully constructed structure, which is second to none. The stadium is dedicated to the nearly 200,000 Texans who fought in World War I. The field is named in honor of legendary UT head football coach Darrell K. Royal, who guided the 'Horns' to three National Championships. Since opening day, Texas has enjoyed a remarkable home winning percentage, which includes more than their share of historic wins.

The first game played at the stadium was against Baylor University on November 8, 1924. The dedication game took place against Texas A&M on Thanksgiving Day 1924, which resulted in a 7-0 Texas win. Stadium improvements, which have taken place at the facility throughout the years, have enabled the Texas program to stay at or near the top.

There are many unique features to the Longhorn playing facility, but none more unique than standing in Memorial Stadium and listening to 80,000+ fans sing "The Eyes of Texas" before opening kick off. That is something words can't express.

NICKNAME: Longhorns
MASCOT: Bevo
PLAYING SURFACE: Grass
SEATING CAPACITY: 80,082
CURRENT HEAD COACH: Mack Brown
NOTABLE PLAYERS/COACHES: Players: Bobby Layne, Tommy Nobis, Earl Campbell, Brad Schearer, Kenneth Sims, Ricky Williams, and Major Applewhite. **Coaches:** Dana X. Bible, Darrell K. Royal, Mack Brown.

TEXAS A&M

Kyle Field (1927), College Station, Texas

Loud, enthusiastic, and extremely loyal are words, which aptly describe Texas A&M fans that pack Kyle Field. Nobody circles the wagons like Aggie fans, and Kyle Field may well be the toughest place to play for opposing teams. Since current head coach R.C. Slocum took over the A&M program in 1989, the Aggies are all but unbeatable at home, winning more than 90% of the time.

Edwin Jackson Kyle Field is home to what many consider the best fans in all of college football. The Aggie faithful are affectionately known as the "12th Man". Named after a former Dean of Agriculture at A&M, Kyle Field was first built in 1927. Since then, seating capacity has risen due to stadium enlargements in 1929, 67, 80, and 1997. Kyle Field boasts mammoth three deck stands on the east and west side, which helps contain the deafening crowd noise.

From Homer Norton to Paul Bear Bryant and his "Junction Boys", the A&M football program is steeped in football tradition.

If you want a taste of what Texas A&M is all about, then attend one of their explosive "prep rallies", which are held the night before every home football game at Kyle Field. Even at the "prep rallies", Kyle Field is packed with electric fans.

NICKNAME: Aggies
MASCOT: Reveille
PLAYING SURFACE: Grass
SEATING CAPACITY: 80,650
CURRENT HEAD COACH: R.C. Slocum
NOTABLE PLAYERS/COACHES: **Players:** Jack Pardee, John David Crow, Sam Adams. **Coaches:** Homer Norton, Paul "Bear" Bryant, Gene Stallings, Jackie Sherrill, R.C. Slocum.

Photographs courtesy of Texas A&M

Photographs courtesy of Texas Tech Media Relations

TEXAS TECH

Jones Stadium (1947), Lubbock, Texas

Built in 1947 with an original seating capacity of 27,000, Clifford B. and Audrey Jones Stadium has been a model of architectural excellence and durability throughout the years. Texas Tech opened Jones Stadium in style, beating Hardin-Simmons 14-6 in 1947. Enlargements to stadium capacity took place in '59, as seating was raised to 41,500, and also in '72, bringing it to its current level of 50,500-seats.

The facility is also home to some of the best stadium amenities, which include; a scoreboard and message center, immaculate player locker rooms, a beautiful playing surface, luxurious coaches and administrative offices, and a gorgeous "Letterman's Lounge Building". Jones Stadium also houses a 10-foot bronze statue of their mascot, a Masked Red Raider on horseback.

The fans that religiously attend home games are knowledgeable, loyal, enthusiastic, and provide a home field advantage which few schools can match.

Though Texas Tech has enjoyed much success in Jones Stadium throughout the years, relatively new Head Coach Mike Leach will undoubtedly raise the level of competition to new heights, while Red Raider fans will continue to support their beloved program.

NICKNAME:	Red Raiders
MASCOT:	Raider Red & The Masked Rider
PLAYING SURFACE:	Artificial Turf
SEATING CAPACITY:	50,500
CURRENT HEAD COACH:	Mike Leach

NOTABLE PLAYERS/COACHES: Players: Zach Thomas, Byron Hanspard. **Coaches:** Dell Morgan, Jim Carlen, Spike Dykes.

ALABAMA-BIRMINGHAM (UAB)

ARMY

CINCINNATI

EAST CAROLINA

HOUSTON

LOUISVILLE

MEMPHIS

SOUTHERN MISSISSIPPI

TEXAS CHRISTIAN UNIVERSITY

TULANE

Courtesy of Division of Parks Services City of Memphis

CONFERENCE USA

Though Conference U.S.A. doesn't have the overall history as does the Big 10 Conference or the SEC, it more than makes up for it with an exciting and well-contested brand of football. The programs, which make up Conference U.S.A., are very competitive with the bigger conferences, while making it a habit of consistently beating some of the nation's elite teams year in and year out.

The stadiums, which are steeped in history and tradition, are well constructed and offer each of their home teams a unique home field advantage. Conference U.S.A. fans are also very instrumental in the success of the league as well as their individual teams.

From gorgeous and historic Michie Stadium at West Point to the Liberty Bowl in Memphis, Conference U.S.A. can be very proud of their stadiums and the memories, which these venues have been home to, throughout the history of college football.

ALABAMA-BIRMINGHAM (UAB)

Legion Field (1927), Birmingham, Alabama

Legion Field stands as a memorial to all Americans killed in action, and is named in honor of the American Legion. Though Alabama-Birmingham plays their home games in historic Legion Field, college football fans may know that the stadium is also the second home for the Alabama Crimson Tide football program.

Throughout the years the Blazers have experienced a good deal of success inside the 82,000-seat stadium, which is one of the most gorgeous facilities in the entire south. Legion Field offers UAB a dominating home field presence along with all the amenities of a top-shelf program. Built in the mid-1920's, Legion Field boasts some of the nation's top stadium medical personnel, permanent lighting, thousands of comfortable chair-back seats with unobstructed views of the playing surface, and a huge press box.

With the possible exception of Army, UAB plays their home games in one of the most historic facilities in the entire conference. Legion Field has been home to many great players, coaches, teams, and games that any football fan would do well to see a game there at least once. Coach Watson Brown once again has an exciting and enthusiastic team, which could challenge for the conference title and bring large crowds to Legion Field.

NICKNAME: Blazers
MASCOT: Blaze
PLAYING SURFACE: Grass
SEATING CAPACITY: 82,000
CURRENT HEAD COACH: Watson Brown
NOTABLE PLAYERS/COACHES: Players: Josh Evans, Izell Reese. **Coaches:** Watson Brown.

Photo credit: Associated Press, AP

ARMY

Michie Stadium (1924), West Point, New York

There are few places, if any, which are as majestic and beautiful as Michie Stadium, located at West Point. Army opened Michie Stadium with an impressive win over St. Louis University, October 4, 1924. Dedication game came a month later, November 15th, when Army battled Columbia University to a 14-14 tie.

The stadium was built on the banks of the Hudson River. Named for Dennis Mahan Michie, the man who instituted the playing of football at West Point in the late 19th century, the facility may be home to the most gorgeous setting in all of college football.

In 1962, the east stands of the stadium became a permanent fixture, while the upper decks were added in '69. In 1977, artificial turf was installed, but was replaced in 1984 by super-turf. Artificial turf was re-installed in 1992.

For many years Michie Stadium had been one of the most devastating places to play for opposing teams. Army enjoyed a home-winning streak of 42 games from 1941-50, and can boast nearly 30 seasons of undefeated home play.

NICKNAME:	The Black Knights
MASCOT:	The Black Knight
PLAYING SURFACE:	Artificial Turf
SEATING CAPACITY:	39,929
CURRENT HEAD COACH:	Todd Berry

NOTABLE PLAYERS/COACHES: Players: Doc Blanchard, Glenn Davis, Pete Dawkins. **Coaches:** Red Blaik, Jim Young.

Photographs courtesy of Army

CINCINNATI

Nippert Stadium (1924), Cincinnati, Ohio

The University of Cincinnati is not just a perennial basketball power. The football team, under Head Coach Rick Minter, has proven to be a feisty and downright scary team to play for some of the nations top schools.

The Bearcats have played their home games at Nippert Stadium since 1902. The only Division 1-A facility which is older than Cincinnati's Nippert Stadium, is Georgia Tech's Bobby Dodd Stadium.

The field is named after Arch Carson, a gentleman who helped start football at Cincinnati in 1885. He was a player and later a physical education director at Cincinnati. In 1916, construction began on a permanent structure, which is made out of a beautiful blend of concrete and brick.

In 1923, Cincinnati played Hanover College under the lights, which may have been the Midwest's first collegiate football night game. James Gamble Nippert, who the stadium honors with its name, played for Cincinnati in the early 1920's. Tragically, he suffered a spike injury while playing for the Bearcats, which would ultimately result in his death.

In 1992, Nippert Stadium underwent a very expensive renovation, which ushered in a gorgeous press box, a new scoreboard and lighting system, and immaculate VIP lounges.

NICKNAME: Bearcats
MASCOT: The Bearcat
PLAYING SURFACE: Artificial Turf
SEATING CAPACITY: 35,000
CURRENT HEAD COACH: Rick Minter
NOTABLE PLAYERS/COACHES: **Players:** James Gamble Nippert, Vaughn Booker, Robert Tate. **Coaches:** Sid Gillman, Rick Minter.

Courtesy of University of Cincinnati Sports Information

EAST CAROLINA

Dowdy-Ficklen Stadium (1963), Greenville, North Carolina

Dowdy-Ficklen Stadium is the beautiful home of the East Carolina University football team. Opened in 1963, Dowdy-Ficklen is named in honor of tobacco pioneer James Skinner Ficklen and Ron Dowdy. East Carolina University dedicated the stadium September 21, 1963, by beating Wake Forest 20-10. At its opening, Dowdy-Ficklen's capacity was less then 20,000-seats, but after renovations in 1968 and 1978, seating increased to 48,000.

The stadium offers spectators one of the South's most comfortable and gorgeous settings for college football. Modern lighting and scoreboard systems, as well as a luxurious and spacious press box, put Dowdy-Ficklen near the top of the list in stadium amenities.

The East Carolina University football team plays in a fun, fan friendly, and comfortable facility. It is now and has been a tough place to play for opposing teams. Over the past ten seasons, Head Coach Steve Logan and his teams have been almost unbeatable at home.

There are few places in Conference U.S.A, which can captivate the fan with the aura of college football like Dowdy-Ficklen.

NICKNAME: Pirates
MASCOT: Pee-Dee
PLAYING SURFACE: Grass
SEATING CAPACITY: 48,000
CURRENT HEAD COACH: Steve Logan
NOTABLE PLAYERS/COACHES: Players: Terry Long, Robert Jones, Jeff Blake. **Coaches:** Pat Dye, Steve Logan.

HOUSTON

Robertson Stadium (1937), Houston, Texas

Robertson Stadium has once again become home for the University of Houston football team. Built in 1941 by the Houston Independent School District and the Works Progress Administration, Robertson Stadium was originally named the Houston Public School Stadium.

During its first five seasons, the stadium was home to Houston area high school football games. The University of Houston's first football game in the facility took place September 21, 1946, against Southwestern Louisiana. This was home for the Cougars until 1950 when Houston moved their games over to Rice Stadium. Since the early 1950's, the Cougars have called Rice Stadium, the Astrodome, and Robertson Stadium home. The Cougars returned to their current home in 1995, which is named in honor of Corbin J. Robertson, a former Athletics Committee Chairman and member of the Houston board of Regents.

During the Cougars absence, the stadium underwent many upgrades and even a name change. Before the facility took the name Robertson in 1980, it had been called Jeppesen Stadium since 1958, after the Houston Independent School District renamed it. It became a mecca for track and field events for the university while the football team played in the Astrodome. Major changes in 1983 and 89 have made the facility comfortable and modern.

NICKNAME: Cougars
MASCOT: Shasta
PLAYING SURFACE: Grass
SEATING CAPACITY: 32,000
CURRENT HEAD COACH: Dana Dimel
NOTABLE PLAYERS/COACHES: **Players:** Andre Ware, David & Jimmy Klingler. **Coaches:** Bill Yeomen, Dana Dimel.

Courtesy of University of Houston Sports Information

Courtesy of Louisville Sports Information Photography & Design

LOUISVILLE

Papa John's Cardinal Stadium (1998), Louisville, Kentucky

The Louisville football program has been elevated due to the construction of the 63 million-dollar, Papa John's Cardinal Stadium.

This multi-faceted home of the Cardinals is one of the best facilities in the entire nation. The stadium is home to a huge and luxurious press box, as well as a gargantuan 100-yard long Brown & Williamson Club, which houses banquets and parties. Another highlight of the stadium is the Cardinal Football Complex which is home to a number of modern amenities.

Though the current seating capacity at Papa John's Cardinal Stadium is a very impressive 42,000 seats (all of which are chair back), the facility was built so it could be renovated to hold over 80,000 seats with no problems.

Even though the Cardinal football program is the obvious primary attendant of the new stadium, the facility has been home to many other events in its short history. In May of 1999, George Strait entertained more than 51,000 fans as did Reba McEntire in 2000. In the summer of 2000, the Billy Graham Crusade graced Papa John's Cardinal Stadium, where Mr. Graham ministered to more than 57,000 people in one night.

NICKNAME: Cardinals
MASCOT: Cardinal Bird
PLAYING SURFACE: Grass
SEATING CAPACITY: 42,000
CURRENT HEAD COACH: John L. Smith
NOTABLE PLAYERS/COACHES: **Players:** John Unitas, Tom Jackson, Ray Buchanan, Ted Washington, Sam Madison, Chris Redman. **Coaches:** Lee Corso, Howard Schellenberger, John L. Smith.

MEMPHIS

Liberty Bowl Memorial Stadium (1965), Memphis, Tennessee

Constructed in the shape of a huge sombrero, the Liberty Bowl is a fine example of architectural ingenuity. Built in 1965, the Liberty Bowl Memorial Stadium/Rex Dockery Field has long been home to Tiger football.

The Liberty Bowl is memorialized for the men and women who fought in either WWI, WWII, or the Korean Conflict. The field is named in memory of former Tiger football coach Rex Dockery, who lost his life in a plane crash.

The Liberty Bowl's facilities have been upgraded to include a gorgeous prescription turf field, a giant scoreboard and sound system, a new lighting system, luxurious sky-seats, as well as updated restroom and renovated concession facilities. All seating allows spectators unobstructed views of the entire field.

The Liberty Bowl is not just the home to the University of Memphis football team. The facility also hosts a number of events throughout the year. One of those events is the actual Liberty Bowl game, which is played every December between the champions of the Mountain West Conference and Conference U.S.A.

NICKNAME: Tigers
MASCOT: Pouncer
PLAYING SURFACE: Grass
SEATING CAPACITY: 62,380
CURRENT HEAD COACH: Tommy West
NOTABLE PLAYERS/COACHES: **Players:** Dave Casinelli, Paul "Skeeter" Gowen, Steve Matthews, Isaac Bruce. **Coaches:** Bill Murphy, Rex Dockery

Courtesy of Division of Parks Services City of Memphis

SOUTHERN MISSISSIPPI
M. M. Roberts Stadium (1976), Hattiesburg, Mississippi

The University of Southern Mississippi football team plays its home games at M.M. Roberts Stadium. This beautiful and spacious facility has a unique history, which dates back to 1932. In 1934, the stadium hosted its first football game under the lights, as Southwestern Louisiana was beaten 12-6.

Shortly after, work was done to expand the facility as the East Stadium Dormitory was built, marking the first permanent part of what is now Roberts Stadium. The West Stadium Dormitory was built in 1950, adding an additional 7,500-seats.

M.M. Roberts Stadium was dedicated in 1976 in honor of the man who had been a member of the Board of Trustees of State Institutions of Higher Learning. Since then, Southern Mississippi has furthered the development of the stadium by making upgrades to already existing facilities.

The Southern Miss football team consistently plays in front of 30,000+ spectators for home games, which is a tribute to their loyal support. One of the largest crowds to ever see a home game inside Roberts Stadium took place September 1989, when the Golden Eagles played Mississippi State University. On that day over 34,000 fans came to support Southern Miss as they battled the Bulldogs.

NICKNAME:	Golden Eagles
MASCOT:	Seymour
PLAYING SURFACE:	Grass
SEATING CAPACITY:	33,000
CURRENT HEAD COACH:	Jeff Bower

NOTABLE PLAYERS/COACHES: Players: Brett Favre, T.J. Slaughter, Patrick Surtain. **Coaches:** Thad "Pie" Vann, Bobby Collins, Jeff Bower.

Photo credit: King Photography

Autumn's Cathedrals 55

TEXAS CHRISTIAN UNIVERSITY

Amon G. Carter Stadium (1929), Fort Worth, Texas

Named for the man who is credited for ushering TCU into the national spotlight and a noted publisher for the Fort Worth Star-Telegram, Amon G. Carter Stadium is a gorgeous venue to watch college football. Built in 1929 with an impressive capacity of 22,000-seats, the stadium was dedicated a year later when TCU played Arkansas.

As TCU football grew, stadium upgrades took place with great regularity. There were expansions to raise seating capacity in 1948, '51, '53, and '56. More changes to the facility included, the construction of a luxury press box in 1956, as well as a contemporary lighting system, built in 1983. For the comfort of the fans, aluminum seating was installed for much of the stadium in 1985, while in 1992 sound and scoreboard systems were implemented.

A number of home games surpassed the 44,000-attendance level, with a couple of those games bringing in more than 47,000 fans. One particular game of note took place in 1984 against the University of Texas. That day, 47,280 fans packed Carter Stadium to watch the Horned Frogs battle the Longhorns.

NICKNAME: Horned Frogs
MASCOT: The Horned Frog
PLAYING SURFACE: Grass
SEATING CAPACITY: 44,008
CURRENT HEAD COACH: Gary Patterson
NOTABLE PLAYERS/COACHES: **Players:** Sammy Baugh, Davey O'Brien, Bob Lilly, Ryan Tucker, LaDainian Tomlinson. **Coaches:** Leo "Dutch" Meyer, Abe Martin, Dennis Francione.

Photographs courtesy of TCU Media Relations

TULANE

Louisiana Superdome (1975), New Orleans, Louisiana

Built in 1975, the Louisiana Superdome is the celebrated home of the Tulane Greenwave football team. The stadium sits a few miles away from the Tulane campus, offering the football program a top shelf venue to play their home games.

The Superdome was the largest enclosed stadium ever built, when construction was complete in 1975. Sitting on approximately 13 acres, the Superdome also boasts the largest steel roof anywhere in the world.

Not only is the Superdome the imposing home for the Green Wave football program, it also has hosted a handful of Super Bowls, Final Fours, a political National Convention, as well as the National Football League's New Orleans Saints.

The additions of numerous message centers and scoreboards throughout the facility have helped to modernize the Superdome. Restroom and concession facilities are top of the line, as well as the relatively new "SuperVision" television screen.

Over the past few years the Tulane football program has enjoyed much success inside the friendly confines of the Dome. That success included a 1998 Conference Championship, which helped propel the Green Wave to a top ten national ranking.

NICKNAME:	Green Wave
MASCOT:	Rip Tide
PLAYING SURFACE:	Artificial Turf
SEATING CAPACITY:	69,767
CURRENT HEAD COACH:	Chris Scelfo

NOTABLE PLAYERS/COACHES: Players: Bill Banker, Gerald Dalrymple, Monk Simons, Shaun King. **Coaches:** Bernie Bierman, Mack Brown, Tommy Bowden.

CENTRAL FLORIDA

CONNECTICUT

NAVY

NOTRE DAME

SOUTH FLORIDA

TROY STATE

UTAH STATE

INDEPENDENTS CONFERENCE

Over the last decade, major football programs that were once known as Independents such as Penn State, Miami and Florida State have found homes in conferences. Still, there are a few schools whose football programs have no allegiance to any league. Those Division 1A programs, which are still known as Independents are: Central Florida, South Florida, Connecticut, Utah State, the Naval Academy and, of course, Notre Dame. Also included is Troy State, which will be an Independent member in 2002.

Though these Independent schools do not make up a conference, I felt it prudent to write about their individual stadium history within the same section.

Each one of the six Independent programs has a unique story to tell concerning their football stadium. Though many of the venues aren't as rich in tradition, history, and lore as Notre Dame or the the Naval Academy, each facility does promote a classy and exciting atmosphere for college football. Fan loyalty and commitment at each school help make every stadium an imposing place to play for visiting teams.

CENTRAL FLORIDA

Florida Citrus Bowl (1936), Orlando, Florida

The Central Florida Golden Knight football team plays in one of the prettiest and most luxurious stadiums, the Florida Citrus Bowl. Orlando Stadium, as it was first called, was part of President Franklin Roosevelt's Works Progress Administration or (WPA), which provided unemployed individuals work during the depression. The original cost of the facility was an incredible $115,000.

On January 1, 1947, Catawba and Maryville played in the first game at the newly named Tangerine Bowl. A crowd of nearly 9,000 showed up to watch Catawba win handily 31-6.

Renovations in 1952, '68, '74, '76, and '89 have elevated seating in the facility to its current level. Other additions to this gorgeous stadium include a gigantic and luxurious press box; concrete ramp towers at each corner of the stadium, huge locker rooms, and private luxury suites. In 1983 the Tangerine Bowl was renamed the Florida Citrus Bowl.

Every January, the stadium is home to the always-exciting Citrus Bowl game, which pits teams from the Big Ten Conference against those from the Southeastern Conference.

One of the biggest crowds to see a game in the Florida Citrus Bowl was January 1, 1991 when 72,328 fans saw Georgia Tech beat Nebraska 45-24 to win a share of the National Championship.

As of the 2002 season, Central Florida moved to the Mid American Conference, East Division.

NICKNAME: Golden Knights
MASCOT: Nitro
PLAYING SURFACE: Grass
SEATING CAPACITY: 70,349
CURRENT HEAD COACH: Mike Kruczek
NOTABLE PLAYERS/COACHES: **Players:** Cornell Green, Shawn Jefferson, Daunte Culpepper. **Coaches:** Mike Kruczek.

Photos by Paul Chapman. Courtesy of UCF Sports Information

Courtesy of University of Connecticut

CONNECTICUT

Memorial Stadium (1953), East Hartford, Connecticut

The Huskies, who are still in their Division 1A football-infancy, are looking to elevate themselves to a more competitive level. The team is planning to move their home games to the gorgeous 40,000-plus-seat Rentscler Field, situated in East Hartford. Until then, the Huskies will continue to play home contests in historic Memorial Stadium.

The first game Connecticut played in the facility took place October 10, 1953 as UCONN beat St. Lawrence University. The largest crowd to witness a Connecticut home game was in 1970, when 16,464 spectators packed Memorial Stadium to watch the Huskies crush Rhode Island 33-12.

The facility offers the Connecticut football players and spectators many top-notch services including: comfortable seating, a permanent lighting system, a contemporary scoreboard with message center, along with spacious locker rooms and storage areas.

While the Connecticut players and fans anxiously await their new home in East Hartford, they will no doubt continue to embrace Memorial Stadium by showing up for home games in mass numbers to cheer on their beloved Huskies.

NICKNAME:	Huskies
MASCOT:	Jonathan
PLAYING SURFACE:	Grass
SEATING CAPACITY:	16,200
CURRENT HEAD COACH:	Randy Edsall

NOTABLE PLAYERS/COACHES: Players: Brian Kozlowski. **Coaches:** Skip Holtz, Randy Edsall.

NAVY

Navy-Marine Corps Memorial Stadium (1959)
Annapolis, Maryland

If you want tradition, the Navy-Marine Corps Memorial Stadium is the place to be. Inside this beautiful stadium are memorials, dedications, and quotes made for past and present Naval and Marine warriors. Constructed for the 1959 season, the facility is in honor of all who have served and will serve in the Navy and Marine Corps.

The first game played in the Navy-Marine Corps Memorial Stadium was also dedication day, September 26, 1959, when the Midshipmen beat William & Mary 29-2.

Over-capacity crowds of up to 35,000, have consistently packed Memorial Stadium throughout the years.

President Eisenhower visited the stadium for the Navy-Villanova contest in 1960, and Jimmy Carter was there on November 12, 1977, to witness Navy's defeat of Georgia Tech.

The Stadium Complex includes: the gorgeous 30,000-seat facility, which houses the immaculate Admiral Thomas J. Hamilton Locker Room Complex and Walk of Fame, an updated 12,000 square foot locker room, the Joe Bellino Auditorium, as well as the Roger Staubach locker room. Memorial Stadium also boasts plaques commemorating legendary Naval and Marine battles on both the east and west sides of the facility.

NICKNAME: Midshipmen
MASCOT: Bill the Goat
PLAYING SURFACE: Artificial Turf
SEATING CAPACITY: 30,000
CURRENT HEAD COACH: Paul Johnson
NOTABLE PLAYERS/COACHES: **Players:** Joe Bellino, Roger Staubach, Napolean McCallum. **Coaches:** Eddie Erdelatz, Wayne Hardin, George Welsh.

Top: Photo courtesy of Navy

Photo credit: David Wallace

NOTRE DAME

Notre Dame Stadium (1930), South Bend, Indiana

Many consider Notre Dame Stadium to be the symbol for all college football stadiums. Quite possibly, no other venue has housed as many legendary players, coaches, teams, or games, as Notre Dame Stadium.

When the facility was built in 1930, it was patterned after the University of Michigan's Stadium. The structure is made up of more than 2-million bricks, over 15,000 cubic yards of concrete, and 400 tons of steel. Legendary coach Knute Rockne oversaw much of the design and construction of the facility.

When the stadium opened against Southern Methodist University, its capacity was an impressive 54,400-seats. Dedication game, October 11, 1930, against the Naval Academy, was won by the Fighting Irish 26-2. Over the years the team has been all but unbeatable in their stadium, going undefeated at home in nearly 30 seasons. From November 21, 1942 to October 7, 1950, the Irish failed to lose a game at home, an impressive span of 28 straight wins.

In 1996, upgrades and enlargements to already top-notch facilities solidified Notre Dame's commitment to modernize an historic facility. The changes included: raising seating capacity, the implementing of contemporary message centers and scoreboards, as well as the construction of a luxurious and spacious three-tiered press box.

NICKNAME: Fighting Irish
MASCOT: The Leprechaun
PLAYING SURFACE: Grass
SEATING CAPACITY: 80,012
CURRENT HEAD COACH: Tyrone Willingham
NOTABLE PLAYERS/COACHES: Players: Angelo Bertelli, Johnny Lujack, Leon Hart, Paul Hornung. John Huarte, Tim Brown. **Coaches:** Knute Rockne, Frank Leahy, Ara Parseghian, Dan Devine, Lou Holtz.

SOUTH FLORIDA

Raymond James Stadium (1998), Tampa Bay, Florida

The state of the art Raymond James Stadium is not only home to the Bulls of South Florida University, but to the NFL's Tampa Bay Buccaneers.

Raymond James Stadium is a jewel of a facility. It opened September 20, 1998, as the Buccaneers beat their long time rival Chicago Bears, 27-15. The stadium is named in honor of the Raymond James Investment Firm.

Designed by the HOK Sports Facilities Group, the facility was constructed with the spectators first in mind. More than 52,000 of the 66,000 seats are of the chair back variety, which are designed for the general spectator. The other 14,000 chairs are either in the luxury box suites or are wheelchair-accessible.

The stadium boasts one of the nicest playing surfaces in all of sports, spacious locker rooms, and a monster Instant Replay Board. But the most noticeable aspect of Raymond James Stadium is the life-size pirate ship, which graces the north end zone.

NICKNAME:	Bulls
MASCOT:	Rocky the Bull
PLAYING SURFACE:	Grass
SEATING CAPACITY:	66,000
CURRENT HEAD COACH:	Jim Leavitt

NOTABLE PLAYERS/COACHES: Players: Kenyatta Jones, Bill Gramatica. **Coaches:** Jim Leavitt

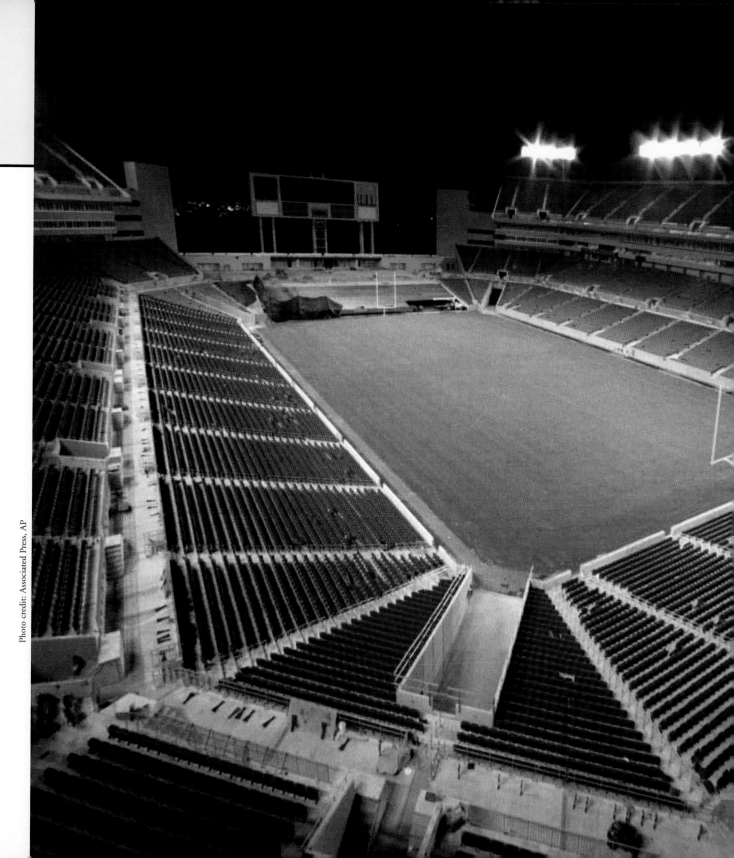

Photo credit: Associated Press, AP

Courtesy of Troy State

TROY STATE

Memorial Stadium (1950), Troy, Alabama

The Troy State Trojans were in a precarious position at the start of the 2001-football season. They did not officially hold a Division 1-A status, though they had scheduled a number of nationally ranked 1-A teams. For the 2001-season, they played their games in a transitional limbo. The Trojans will be an Independents' member in 2002 making them the 117th program on college football's highest level.

They play their home games in Memorial Stadium; named in honor of the residents in Pike County, Alabama, as well as the students of Troy State University who served so valiantly in World War II.

The Trojans played their first game at Memorial Stadium September 16, 1950 against Southeastern Louisiana. The stadium was not officially dedicated until homecoming day, November 4, 1950.

The CEO of HealthSouth, Richard M. Scrushy, donated close to $4-million towards the most recent renovation, which saw capacity rise to its current level. It is home to chair-back seating, a number of concession stands, and luxury boxes. The layout of the facility also allows for increased capacity.

The Trojans jump to Division 1-A will be tough, but Memorial Stadium will undoubtedly give Troy State a good chance of winning a number of games.

NICKNAME: Trojans
MASCOT: T-Roy
PLAYING SURFACE: Grass
SEATING CAPACITY: 17,500+
CURRENT HEAD COACH: Larry Blakeney
NOTABLE PLAYERS/COACHES: **Players:** Marcus Spriggs, Rod Walker, Al Lucas. **Coaches:** Larry Blakeney.

UTAH STATE

Romney Stadium (1969), Logan, Utah

Since 1968, E.L. "Dick" Romney Stadium has been the home for the Utah State Aggie football team. The first game played in this beautiful facility was September 14, 1968, when Utah State defeated, New Mexico State University 28-12. Dedication day came a year later, September 27, 1969.

The stadium was named for the winningest coach in Aggie history, E.L. "Dick" Romney.

Original capacity at Romney Stadium was just over 20,000-seats, but in 1980, expansion efforts raised capacity to its current level of 30,257. The stands on the east and west sides of the facility, which uniquely start at the 15-yard line, are raised eight feet above the playing surface. The stadium also boasts a remodeled and luxurious glass press box, which includes a number of television sets.

Utah State has had great success at home, registering close to 25 winning seasons. The Aggies have also enjoyed impressive fan support throughout its 32-year history at Romney Stadium, including a record high 31,287 single game attendance record for the 1994 game against rival Utah.

NICKNAME:	Aggies
MASCOT:	Big Blue
PLAYING SURFACE:	Artificial Turf
SEATING CAPACITY:	30,257
CURRENT HEAD COACH:	Mike Dennehy

NOTABLE PLAYERS/COACHES: **Players:** Merlin Olson, Johndale Carty, Micah Knorr. **Coaches:** E.L. Romney.

Courtesy of Athletic Media Relations Utah State University

East Division
AKRON
BOWLING GREEN
BUFFALO
KENT STATE
MARSHALL
MIAMI (OH)
OHIO

West Division
BALL STATE
CENTRAL MICHIGAN
EASTERN MICHIGAN
NORTHERN ILLINOIS
TOLEDO
WESTERN MICHIGAN

Photo credit: Gary Shook

MID AMERICAN CONFERENCE

The Mid-American Conference is the nation's largest and is one of the most competitive. Every team in both the East and West divisions are fierce competitors and play a tough brand of football.

As the conference has grown into the national spotlight over the past few years, the stadiums in which the teams play have also expanded in a like manner to accommodate the increased exposure.

Mid-American Conference football teams play in facilities, which are unique, as well as historical. They are fan-friendly, comfortable, promote an honest and classy college football setting, and have been home to more than their share of great players and teams.

*Due to the complications of adjusting the conferences after this book went to press, we are listing new changes for the 2002 season here.

- Bowling Green moves to the West division.
- Central Florida moves from the Independents to the East division.

Autumn's Cathedrals 67

AKRON

Rubber Bowl (1940), Akron, Ohio

The Rubber Bowl has been the beautiful home for the Akron Zips for over 60 years. Dedicated in August 1940 in front of an estimated 37,000 spectators, the Zips played their first home game in the facility the following October against Western Reserve. Akron's first win in the Bowl came November 11, 1940 when they beat Kent 23-7.

The site the stadium now sits on was once a recreational area, which was carved out of the side of a hill. Six years later, in 1937, two Akron citizens raised enough money to build what would become the Rubber Bowl.

After expansions in 1971, '73, '83, '91, and '95, the Rubber Bowl received a new lighting system, an updated scoreboard, the implementation of fiberglass seating, as well as a unique paint job. It also boasts one of the Midwest's nicest playing fields.

The stadium is called upon for a number of uses, which include: high school football games, soccer matches, and even professional sporting events.

The Akron Zips have enjoyed an impressive home record since the early 1940s, and have no intention of letting their home field advantage go to waste. The Rubber Bowl is one of the Mid-American Conference's nicest facilities.

NICKNAME: Zips
MASCOT: Zippy
PLAYING SURFACE: Artificial Turf
SEATING CAPACITY: 35,202
CURRENT HEAD COACH: Lee Owens
NOTABLE PLAYERS/COACHES: **Players:** Victor Green, Jason Taylor. **Coaches:** Gerry Faust.

Courtesy of the University of Akron

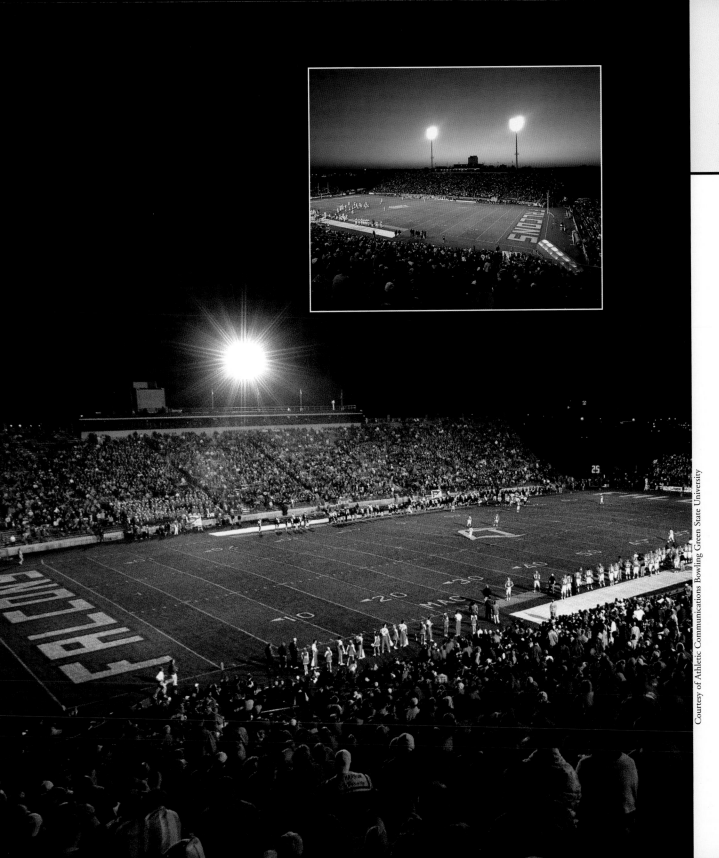

Courtesy of Athletic Communications Bowling Green State University

BOWLING GREEN

Doyt L. Perry Stadium (1966), Bowling Green, Ohio

Doyt L. Perry was one of the most successful coaches in the history of college football, earning a .855 winning percentage at Bowling Green University during the 1950's and 60's.

Built in 1966, Perry Stadium's original capacity was 23,272-seats, but the expansion of '82, elevated seating to its current level 30,599. The first game played in the facility took place October 1, 1966 when the Falcons beat Dayton 13-0.

Bowling Green has enjoyed a marvelous winning record of close to 68% at home. This success can be attributed to many things, which include: great coaching, talented teams, and fan support.

One of the most well-attended games in stadium history took place October 8, 1983, when a then conference record 33,527 fans packed the facility to watch Bowling Green play Toledo.

Doyt L. Perry Stadium comes complete with luxury box seats, a Presidents box, and top of the line training rooms, departmental offices, updated restroom and concession facilities, as well as contemporary locker rooms.

NICKNAME: Falcons
MASCOT: Freida & Freddie Falcon
PLAYING SURFACE: Grass
SEATING CAPACITY: 30,599
CURRENT HEAD COACH: Urban Meyer
NOTABLE PLAYERS/COACHES: Players: Ryan Diepenbrock, Derek Schorejs. **Coaches:** Doyt L. Perry, Denny Stolz, Gary Blackney.

BUFFALO

UB Stadium (1993), Buffalo, New York

The UB Football Stadium sits on the University of Buffalo campus and is one of the most versatile, multi-purpose facilities in the entire Mid-American Conference. Completed just before the 1993 football season, the 23-million dollar complex is home to the University of Buffalo track and field teams as well.

Though the Bulls have only been a Division 1-A football program for a short time, they play in a well-established and very impressive sports facility. The stadium also boasts a number of amenities, including: a number of meeting rooms and administrative offices, two huge and comfortable locker rooms, a state-of-the-art press box, luxury suites, as well as training facilities, and conditioning equipment. The UB Football Stadium already has the service of permanent lights as well as a gorgeous playing field and an equally impressive track.

Though there is great excitement and anticipation surrounding the entire Bull football program, there is just as much enthusiasm shown towards the stadium in which they play. In its short history, the UB Football Stadium has already had the great honor of hosting the 1993 World University Games, as well as the 1998 Division-1 Outdoor Track and Field Championships. The 1998 Championships have the dubious distinction of being the first games contested in western New York.

NICKNAME: Bulls
MASCOT: Victor E Bull & Victoria S Bull
PLAYING SURFACE: Grass
SEATING CAPACITY: 31,000
CURRENT HEAD COACH: Jim Hofher
NOTABLE PLAYERS/COACHES: **Players:** Ed Ellis, Drew Haddad, Noah Burroughs. **Coaches:** Jim Hofher

Courtesy of the University of Buffalo

Courtesy of Sports Information Kent State University

KENT STATE

Dix Stadium (1970), Kent, Ohio

Robert C. Dix Stadium is an impressive, all-around facility named for the man who was a Kent Board of Trustees member for over three decades.

The 30,520-seat stadium was dedicated September 19, 1970 as Kent State played Ohio University. The largest crowd to witness a game at Dix Stadium took place November 11, 1973, as the Golden Flashes battled Miami University in front of 27,363 spectators.

The stadium itself offers players and fans some of the best amenities and facilities found anywhere in the Mid-American Conference. Impressive coaches offices, training rooms, and equipment facilities are found within the West-side stands of the stadium. Dix boasts a spacious press box, which can accommodate a number of media personnel, a luxurious Presidential box, as well as a number of concessions and restroom facilities. One of the best assets of the venue is the beautiful artificial playing surface on which the Golden Flashes play.

NICKNAME: Golden Flashes
MASCOT: Flash
PLAYING SURFACE: Artificial Turf
SEATING CAPACITY: 30,520
CURRENT HEAD COACH: Dean Pees
NOTABLE PLAYERS/COACHES: **Players:** Jack Lambert, O.J. Santiago. **Coaches:** Don James.

MARSHALL

Marshall University Stadium (1991), Huntington, West Virginia

Few programs ever have been able to make the jump from Division 1-AA to 1-A, and be successful. Not only has Marshall been able to make that jump and be competitive, but have simply dominated the Mid-American Conference since joining in 1997.

Marshall University Stadium is as extraordinary as the team that plays there. Opening for play September 7, 1991, it hosted the largest crowd in the entire state of West Virginia. The 33,116 who packed the stadium that day, set an attendance record for the Thundering Herd that still stands. Since the facility opened in the early 90's, Marshall has averaged well over 20,000 fans per game. Before the Thundering Herd entered college football's toughest stage in 1997, Marshall fans were treated to Division 1-AA National Championship games.

Marshall University Stadium is home to a 37-foot high and 54-foot long contemporary scoreboard, a huge, 75-seat press box, 20+ luxury sky suites, and more than 4,300 comfortable chair back seats. There are numerous handicap accommodations throughout the stadium, along with plenty of concession stands and restroom facilities.

NICKNAME:	Thundering Herd
MASCOT:	Marco
PLAYING SURFACE:	Turf
SEATING CAPACITY:	38,016
CURRENT HEAD COACH:	Bob Pruett

NOTABLE PLAYERS/COACHES: Players: Randy Moss, Chad Pennington. **Coaches:** Jim Donnan, Bob Pruett.

Courtesy of Sports Information Marshall University

Courtesy of Miami University

MIAMI (OH)

Yager Stadium (1983), Oxford, Ohio

Dedicated October 1, 1983 in front of what is still the biggest crowd in Stadium history (28,230), Fred C. Yager Stadium has one of the MAC's top home field advantages. The home of the football program carries the name of a Miami graduate who gave generous amounts of money to support the Red Hawk program, and subsequent stadium projects.

The facility comes complete with an enhanced lighting system, impressive grass playing field, along with a number of offices and rooms, including the famous "Cradle of Coaches Room".

Since its opening in 1983, Miami has consistently drawn crowds of over 25,000. The Miami fans have always supported their Red Hawks vigorously, and, in turn, the football program has consistently maintained an impressive home record. Of note, the team played its first night game at home in Yager Stadium against Ball State to open the 1995 season.

There are few places within the Mid-American Conference, which are prettier than this facility. Crowd enthusiasm combined with team execution make watching a game in Yager Stadium one of the finest experiences the conference has to offer.

NICKNAME: Red Hawks
MASCOT: Swoop
PLAYING SURFACE: Grass
SEATING CAPACITY: 30,012
CURRENT HEAD COACH: Terry Hoeppner
NOTABLE PLAYERS/COACHES: **Players:** Ernie Plank, Sheldon White, Travis Prentice. **Coaches:** Sid Gillman, Woody Hayes, Glenn "Bo" Shembechler, Bill Mallory, Dick Crum.

OHIO

Peden Stadium (1929), Athens, Ohio

Peden Stadium offers spectators a unique blend of architecture and beauty. Built in 1929, with a seating capacity of 12,000, the stadium was named for Don C. Peden, one of the founders of the Mid-American Conference, and former school's athletic director of 30 years.

Renovations to the stadium in 1986, '90, and '99, have raised capacity to 25,000-seats. The most recent renovation occurred when "Victory Hill" was created beyond the south endzone in the summer of 2001. The field was lowered, the track removed, and a lower seating section added.

The venue is also home to the Ohio University track teams. A major part of the beautiful stadium complex is the equally noticeable Peden Tower. Built in 1990, the Tower houses a variety of all-purpose rooms. Situated on the southwest corner of the facility is the new Dr. Steve and Kathy Carin Strength & Conditioning Center. This magnificent 10,000 square-foot building is available to all Ohio University athletes. The Center is home to speed training and platform areas, power racks and benches, along with a number of extra amenities.

NICKNAME: Bobcats
MASCOT: The Bobcat
PLAYING SURFACE: Grass
SEATING CAPACITY: 25,000
CURRENT HEAD COACH: Brian Knorr
NOTABLE PLAYERS/COACHES: **Players:** Art Lewis, Dick Grecni. **Coaches:** Bill Hess.

Top right: Ohio University/Rick Fatica

Top left: Ohio University Publications

Courtesy Ohio Athletics/Scott Gardner

BALL STATE

Ball State University Stadium (1967), Muncie, Indiana

The Cardinal's first game in Ball State Stadium took place October 21, 1967. Ball State opened the facility in style, crushing Butler 65-7. Original capacity in the venue was 16,319-seats, but after renovations in 1995, seating was raised to 18,159.

Ball State football teams have never had any problem drawing loyal Cardinal fans. The "Cardinal Crazies" have always supported their teams, bringing in over 17,000 to home contests on more than one occasion. A crowd of 19,320, the largest in stadium history, saw Ball State battle Indiana State in 1978. That same year the Cardinals registered its best overall home attendance mark, bringing in over 85,000 fans.

Though the home of Cardinal football does not have permanent lights, they do boast an impressive number of training facilities and offices for players and coaches. The stadium hosts spacious meeting rooms, updated locker and weight room facilities, and luxurious hospitality areas.

NICKNAME:	Cardinals
MASCOT:	Charlie Cardinal
PLAYING SURFACE:	Grass
SEATING CAPACITY:	22,500
CURRENT HEAD COACH:	Bill Lynch

NOTABLE PLAYERS/COACHES: Players: Blaine Bishop, Brad Maynard. **Coaches:** John Magnabosco, Ray Louthen, Dave McClain, Paul Schudel.

CENTRAL MICHIGAN

Kelly/Shorts Stadium (1972), Mt. Pleasant, Michigan

The Chippewas call Kelly/Shorts Stadium, in Mount Pleasant, Michigan, home. The facility was dedicated November 4, 1972, with a win against Illinois State. It is named after CMU alumnus and generous donor, Perry Shorts, and legendary CMU football coach Kenneth (Bill) Kelly.

Central Michigan has always had loyal support from their fans in their 30-year stadium history. One of the largest crowds to attend a Chippewa home game took place September 18, 1982, when 29,732 fans packed Kelly/Shorts to watch CMU wage war against Bowling Green University.

CMU has accumulated an impressive winning record of 80% in their venue, including a 15-game win streak beginning in 1978, and ending in 1981.

NICKNAME: Chippewas
MASCOT: No Mascot
PLAYING SURFACE: Artificial Turf
SEATING CAPACITY: 30,200
CURRENT HEAD COACH: Mike Debord
NOTABLE PLAYERS/COACHES: **Players:** Brock Gutierrez, Reginald Allen. **Coaches:** Kenneth (Bill) Kelly, Herb Deromedi, Dick Flynn.

Courtesy of Central Michigan University

Photographs courtesy of Eastern Michigan

EASTERN MICHIGAN
Rynearson Stadium (1969), Ypsilanit, Michigan

Rynearson Stadium is home to Eastern Michigan football. Elton J. Rynearson, Sr. was a legendary head coach for the Eagles during his 26-season tenure. At the height of Rynearson's football reign, Eastern Michigan went 40-4-2 from 1925 to 1930.

The stadium opened for football September 27, 1969, as EMU beat the University of Akron 10-3. A month later on October 25, the facility was dedicated as the Eagles played the University of Tampa.

Original capacity of the facility was 15,500-seats, but crowds of more than 22,000 are not uncommon to the Eagles. The biggest crowd in stadium history was September 16, 1995, when 25,009 fans witnessed Eastern Michigan crushing UNLV 51-6.

Rynearson Stadium boasts a number of elaborate amenities, with the addition of an impressive scoreboard, updated concession and restroom facilities, as well as an expanded press box. Both home and visiting locker rooms at the stadium are spacious and are some of the best the Mid-American Conference has to offer.

NICKNAME: Eagles
MASCOT: Swoop the Eagle
PLAYING SURFACE: Artificial Turf
SEATING CAPACITY: 30,200
CURRENT HEAD COACH: Jeff Woodruff
NOTABLE PLAYERS/COACHES: **Players:** Charlie Batch, Lional Dalton, Barry Stokes. **Coaches:** Elton J. Rynearson, Sr., Jim Harkema.

NORTHERN ILLINOIS

Huskie Stadium (1965), DeKalb, Illinois

Huskie Stadium was built in 1965 with an original capacity of 20,257. The first football game played in the facility, which was both the dedication game and homecoming, took place November 6, 1965, against Illinois State University. The Huskie's overpowered the visitors 48-6 behind quarterback Ron Christian.

The venue is not only home to the football program, but to seven other intercollegiate sports as well, including four women's sports.

The facility houses a world class strength complex, locker rooms, sky boxes, a main and auxiliary press box, storage areas, top-notch training amenities. an elevator, classrooms, and an assortment of offices.

The Huskies play on a beautiful artificial turf field, which was first installed in 1969 but has since been re-carpeted. Northern Illinois played on their new turf field September 20, 1969, marking the first major college football game played on an artificial surface in the state of Illinois.

On November 16, 1968, Northern Illinois won its first game against a major football program, beating Bowling Green 7-6. The next great feat came in October of 1990, when they defeated a top 25-program, the Fresno State Bulldogs, 73-18, behind quarterback Stacey Robinson.

NICKNAME: Huskies
MASCOT: Victor-E
PLAYING SURFACE: Artificial Turf
SEATING CAPACITY: 31,000
CURRENT HEAD COACH: Joe Novak
NOTABLE PLAYERS/COACHES: Players: George Bork, Mark Kellar, Stacey Robinson, LeShon Johnson. **Coaches:** Howard Fletcher, Bill Mallory.

Photographs courtesy of the University of Toledo

TOLEDO
Glass Bowl (1937), Toledo, Ohio

The legendary Glass Bowl has been the home for the Toledo Rockets since September 25, 1937, when Toledo crushed Bluffton College 26-0. Original seating capacity was 7,500.

The Stadium was constructed in 1936 by the Works Progress Administration (WPA), without the aide of any machinery, including bulldozers. The federal government paid nearly $275,000 for the project and the city of Toledo added close to $42,000. A huge glass donation from Toledo glass companies for the stadium press box and towers, solidified the stadium's name as the Glass Bowl.

The facility has undergone a major facelift, which has modernized and expanded the stadium to its current state. A gorgeous media tower which seats more than 1,000 has replaced the old wooden press box, while executive seats and a stadium club area have been added. The Bowl is also home to an impressive sports medicine center, strength and conditioning rooms, meeting and equipment rooms, as well as sports offices.

Toledo has a home-field winning record of close to 73% since the 1967 season. From September 20, 1969 to October 7, 1972 the Rockets were literally unbeatable at home, winning 17 straight home games in the midst of a 35-game overall win streak. One of the largest attended games in stadium history occurred in 1994, when 33,040 people packed in to watch Toledo play Indiana State University.

NICKNAME: Rockets
MASCOT: Rocky
PLAYING SURFACE: Grass
SEATING CAPACITY: 26,248
CURRENT HEAD COACH: Tom Amstutz
NOTABLE PLAYERS/COACHES: Players: Gene Swick, Andy McCollum, Kevin Rollins. **Coaches:** Dr. Clarence Wiley Spears, Frank Lauterbur, Jack Murphy.

WESTERN MICHIGAN

Waldo Stadium (1939), Kalamazoo, Michigan

Waldo Stadium was named for Dwight B. Waldo, the first president of WMU. Its original capacity in 1939, was 15,000 seats. It has undergone a few renovations and facelifts, which have raised seating to its current level of 30,200.

In addition to more seats, Waldo Stadium has also remodeled its press box, upgraded and expanded the locker rooms, while installing permanent lights. The stadium is also home to new and comfortable bench and chair back seats, which make watching Western Michigan games a delight.

In the 60+ seasons the facility has been open, the Broncos have never lacked fervent fan support. The highest single game attendance mark in Bronco history occurred in 1989 against Central Michigan University before 33,272 spectators. The implementation of lights at Waldo Stadium has continued to help usher in huge crowds.

Under head coach Gary Darnell the Broncos have been competitive in the MAC and almost unbeatable in Waldo Stadium. There is no reason to believe that the winning tradition will not continue.

NICKNAME: Broncos
MASCOT: Buster
PLAYING SURFACE: Grass
SEATING CAPACITY: 30,200
CURRENT HEAD COACH: Gary Darnell
NOTABLE PLAYERS/COACHES: **Players:** Tom Nutten, Jake Moreland, Robert Sanford. **Coaches:** Merle Schlosser, Al Molde, Gary Darnell.

Black & White photo courtesy of Western Michigan

Photo Credit: Gary Shook

AIR FORCE

BRIGHAM YOUNG

COLORADO STATE

NEVADA (UNLV)

NEW MEXICO

SAN DIEGO STATE

UTAH

WYOMING

Courtesy of University of Utah Sports Information

MOUNTAIN WEST CONFERENCE

Set mostly in the Rocky Mountain region, the Mountain West Conference is one of college football's most competitive new leagues. No conference can match the game-day setting which each of these stadiums offer.

Every school plays in a gorgeous and spacious facility, which has a uniqueness all its own, making every stadium in the Mountain West Conference post-card material. Many of the schools play their football in the foreground of scenic mountain ranges and those that aren't so lucky, play near beaches or casinos.

Although the venues are impressive in appearance, they are tough and sturdy, just like the teams that play in them.

For the last twenty-five years, BYU has been the most competitive football school nationally out of all the teams that comprise the Mountain West Conference. But with the addition of great football coaches like Sonny Lubick, John Robinson, and Fisher DeBerry, the entire conference has been elevated to a higher competition level.

AIR FORCE

Falcon Stadium (1962), Colorado Springs, Colorado

Few places in the nation are as eye opening as the Air Force Academy's Falcon Stadium. Built in 1962 with an original capacity of 40,828-seats, the Falcons opened the stadium September 22, by beating Colorado State University 34-0 in front of 41,350 spectators.

The venue is a gorgeous structure, which is built into the base of the Rocky Mountains at an elevation of 6,620 feet above sea level. Constructed in a bowl shape, the stadium comes complete with an impressive press box, spacious home and visiting locker rooms, new concession and restroom facilities, and one of the conference's best playing surfaces. Every seat allows for unobstructed views of the field so that each spectator is ensured of a quality college game-day experience.

Over the years Falcon Stadium has seen its share of sell-outs and has drawn close to, and even exceeded, the 50,000 spectator plateau. Their record home attendance game was November 18, 1995 when 54,482 fans watched Air Force battle Notre Dame.

NICKNAME:	Falcons
MASCOT:	The Bird
PLAYING SURFACE:	Grass
SEATING CAPACITY:	52,480
CURRENT HEAD COACH:	Fisher DeBerry

NOTABLE PLAYERS/COACHES: Players: Beau & Blaine Morgan, Chad Hennings. **Coaches:** Ben Martin, Ken Hatfield, Fisher DeBerry.

Photographs courtesy of the Air Force Academy

Photo Credit: Todd Warshaw/Allsport

Top: Mark A. Philbrick/BYU

BRIGHAM YOUNG

LaVell Edwards Stadium (1964), Provo, Utah

Built in 1964, the original seating capacity of what is now LaVell Edwards Stadium, was 30,000. Constructed at the base of the Wasatch Mountains, the stadium is arguably the nations prettiest and most complete sporting facility. It holds the conference's highest capacity of more than 65,000-seats. On October 16, 1993, 66,247 people watched BYU battle Notre Dame in what is still one of the largest crowds in stadium history.

Named in honor of legendary football coach LaVell Edwards, the facility offers spectators much more than extraordinary scenery. It is home to a four-level press box, which is widely regarded as the best in the nation. Sitting more than ten stories high, the press box offers the media luxury that is unparalleled. The facility is also home to the impressive Athletic Hall of Fame along with a huge Jurassic Dinosaur collection.

No place in the Mountain West has seen as many great players, games, coaches, and teams, as has the home for BYU football. Known as "Quarterback U" in many circles, BYU is the only team from the Mountain West Conference to have ever won the National Championship, doing so in 1984.

NICKNAME:	Cougars
MASCOT:	Cosmo
PLAYING SURFACE:	Grass
SEATING CAPACITY:	65,000
CURRENT HEAD COACH:	Gary Crowton

NOTABLE PLAYERS/COACHES: Players: Marc Wilson, Jim McMahon, Steve Young, Robbie Bosco, Ty Detmer, Luke Staley. **Coaches:** LaVell Edwards, Gary Crowton.

COLORADO STATE

Hughes Stadium (1968), Fort Collins, Colorado

Hughes Stadium opened September 28, 1968 playing host to North Texas. The Ram's first victory didn't come until opening day the following year when they beat Wichita State.

On open land, set up against the Rocky Mountain foothills, Hughes Stadium, which is named after legendary head football coach Harry Hughes, is one of the best places to be at sunset. Watching the sun set over the Rocky Mountains while sitting inside the facility is a sight which cannot be described.

Since Sonny Lubick has taken over the coaching duties at CSU, the Rams' fans have filled Hughes Stadium many times. In 1994, 32,618 fans witnessed Colorado State beat conference rival San Diego State 19-17. That same year the Rams posted their best overall season attendance record, averaging over 31,000. Since 1968 the Rams have recorded 20+ winning seasons.

Coach Lubick and his staff have elevated the football program to the top of the Mountain West Conference. Perhaps a national championship is not out of the question for the Rams in the near future.

NICKNAME:	Rams
MASCOT:	Cam the Ram
PLAYING SURFACE:	Grass
SEATING CAPACITY:	30,000
CURRENT HEAD COACH:	Sonny Lubick

NOTABLE PLAYERS/COACHES:**Players:** "Fum" McGraw, Greg Myers, Kevin McDougal. **Coaches:** Bob Davis, Harry Hughes, Earle Bruce, Sonny Lubick.

Photographs courtesy of Colorado State University

Photo credit: Steve Spatafore/UNLV   Top: Courtesy of UNLV   Inset: Dave Phillips

NEVADA-LAS VEGAS (UNLV)

Sam Boyd Stadium (1971), Las Vegas, Nevada

Sam Boyd Stadium is home to the annual Las Vegas Bowl as well as the up-and-coming UNLV football Rebels. Built in 1971 for 3.5 million dollars, the 36,800-seat facility can actually accommodate more than 60,000 fans. Opening game was played in the stadium October 23, against Weber State University.

Named for local gaming pioneer, Sam Boyd, the stadium has housed many sporting and entertainment events; rock concerts featuring Paul McCartney and the Eagles, Canadian Football League games, and motor sports and soccer events, featuring the legendary Pele.

Though not considered a huge college football town, the residents of Las Vegas have done an outstanding job of supporting the program. The Rebels consistently draw more than 25,000 fans while packing in more than 30,000 spectators on numerous occasions. Two games against visiting Wisconsin brought in well over 32,000 fans. The first in 1986 when UNLV beat Wisconsin 17-7, and the second in 1995, when an extra 8,000 seats were added.

NICKNAME:	Rebels
MASCOT:	Hey Reb
PLAYING SURFACE:	Grass
SEATING CAPACITY:	36,800
CURRENT HEAD COACH:	John Robinson

NOTABLE PLAYERS/COACHES: Players: Keenan McCardell, Randall Cunningham, Keith Washington. **Coaches:** Harvey Hyde, John Robinson.

Autumn's Cathedrals   85

NEW MEXICO

University Stadium (1960), Albuquerque, New Mexico

University Stadium is beautifully nestled on the campus of the University of New Mexico. Recently upgraded and enlarged, the "new" stadium is head and shoulders above the tiny facility, which was first constructed in 1960.

Though the Lobos have had a shaky football existence at best, they have made major strides in the past five years in elevating the program to respectability. The facility not only has raised its seating capacity considerably, but also has added a number of top-of-the-line amenities. They include a brand new gigantic scoreboard with message center, a number of new concession areas and restroom facilities, upgraded landscaping in and around the stadium, and newly added novelty stands. The Lobos enjoy playing on one of the nicest grass fields in the Mountain West.

September 1, 2001, the Lobos set an all-time University Stadium record by drawing 41,771 fans to their opening game against UTEP. The previous single-game attendance record for the University of New Mexico was 37,156, set in 1997 against the Rice Owls.

The Lobos have risen from the depths of football futility over the past several years and seem intent on strengthening their program. The recently completed upgrades to University Stadium will undoubtedly bring in much-needed talent.

NICKNAME: Lobos
MASCOT: Lobo Louie
PLAYING SURFACE: Grass
SEATING CAPACITY: 43,000
CURRENT HEAD COACH: Rocky Long
NOTABLE PLAYERS/COACHES: **Players:** Stoney Case, Brian Urlacher. **Coaches:** Ted Shipkey, Willis Barnes, Bill Weeks, Dennis Francione.

Photographs courtesy of the University of New Mexico

SAN DIEGO STATE

Qualcomm Stadium (1967), San Diego, California

Since the 1967 season, the Aztec football team has shared their home facilities with the NFL's San Diego Chargers, and Major League Baseball's San Diego Padres, at what is now called Qualcomm Stadium. Originally called San Diego Stadium, it was built at a cost of 27 million dollars. San Diego State's first game in this state-of-the-art facility was September 15, 1967 when they defeated, Tennessee State University 16-8 in front of 45,822 fans.

The stadium was named Jack Murphy Stadium in January of 1981 after the talented columnist of the *San Diego Union*. It boasts a gorgeous playing field, huge and modernized scoreboards and sound systems, a spacious press box, many luxury box suites, updated and comfortable locker rooms, as well as a contemporary lighting system.

San Diego State has a home winning record of over 71%. Fan attendance has been very impressive for the Aztecs, consistently averaging above 30,000 fans per game.

The largest regular season home crowd, 56,737, watched SDSU play rival BYU in 1991. They were treated to a display of offensive firepower as the Aztecs battled the Cougars to a 52-52 draw.

Although Qualcomm has hosted a couple of Super Bowls, it has never lost the aura that surrounds college football.

NICKNAME: Aztecs
MASCOT: Monty Montezuma
PLAYING SURFACE: Grass
SEATING CAPACITY: 71,400
CURRENT HEAD COACH: Tom Craft
NOTABLE PLAYERS/COACHES: Players: Haven Moses, Fred Dryer, Brian Sipe, Rob Awalt, Darnay Scott, Marshall Faulk. **Coaches:** Don Coryell, Denny Stolz, Al Luginbill.

UTAH

Rice-Eccles Stadium (1927), Salt Lake City, Utah

The home of the University of Utah football team is Rice-Eccles Stadium. Built in 1927, the facility is one of the oldest college football stadiums west of the Rocky Mountains. Utah played their first game at its current home against the Colorado Mines in 1927, beating them 44-6. Positioned beautifully on the Utah campus in eastern Salt Lake City with fully unobstructed views of the Wasatch Mountains, Rice Stadium is without a doubt one of college football's most comfortable and scenic football venues.

Along with seating expansion came the implementation of the nation's first "Sport Grass" field, a new press box, added luxury suites and VIP boxes, and a state-of-the-art scoreboard. The stadium also houses the Spence Clark Football Center, home to spacious locker rooms and a band room.

Before the mid-1990 expansions, Utah fans had consistently crowded more than 32,000 fans into the stadium. One of the biggest crowds to attend a Ute home game came in 1982 when 36,250 watched Utah battle BYU.

NICKNAME: Utes
MASCOT: Swoop
PLAYING SURFACE: Sport Grass
SEATING CAPACITY: 45,634
CURRENT HEAD COACH: Ron McBride
NOTABLE PLAYERS/COACHES: **Players:** Scott Mitchell, Jamal Anderson, Luther Ellis, Kevin Dyson, Mike Anderson. **Coaches:** Ike Armstrong, Ray Nagel, Ron McBride.

Photographs courtesy of University of Utah Sports Information

WYOMING

War Memorial Stadium (1950), Laramie, Wyoming

War Memorial Stadium is sturdy, tough, and a "fan friendly" place to watch some of the Mountain West Conference's most exciting football. Built in 1950, and named in honor of WW II veterans from Wyoming, War Memorial Stadium had an original capacity of 20,000 seats.

Set at the nation's highest elevation of 7,220 feet, this venue is beautifully constructed. Pine trees line the outskirts of both end zones, while the east and west grandstands are risen to heights that give fans the feeling of being right on top of the action. The concession and restroom facilities are some of the best the conference has to offer.

The Cowboys have enjoyed immense success at War Memorial, winning over 70% of their games. Since it's opening, War Memorial has averaged 18,000 fans per game with the record being 34,231, set November 10, 1990, against BYU. The season attendance record came in 1990 when 149,625 viewed Cowboy football.

NICKNAME:	Cowboys
MASCOT:	Cowboy Joe
PLAYING SURFACE:	Grass
SEATING CAPACITY:	33,500
CURRENT HEAD COACH:	Vic Koenning

NOTABLE PLAYERS/COACHES: Players: Jay Novacek, Marcus Harris. **Coaches:** Bob Devaney, Lloyd Eaton, Paul Roach, Joe Tiller.

ARIZONA

ARIZONA STATE

CALIFORNIA

OREGON

OREGON STATE

SOUTHERN CALIFORNIA

STANFORD

UCLA

WASHINGTON

WASHINGTON STATE

Courtesy of Washington State University

PACIFIC TEN CONFERENCE

The Pac Ten Conference is back. Steeped in tradition and lore, the Pac-10 took a slight vacation during the late 90's and had no real national title contender, other than UCLA in 1998. The new millenium has seen the rise of old powers, as well as the new, to the top of the national spotlight with the re-emergence of Washington, Washington State, UCLA, USC, Oregon, and Oregon State.

The Pac-10 has always had everything, including: Heisman Trophy winners, national championship teams, memorable players, legendary coaches, and unforgettable games. But this celebrated league is also home to some of the nation's best venues in which to watch college football. From tailgating on boats outside the gorgeous Husky Stadium in Seattle, to the hallowed grounds of UCLA's Rose Bowl; from thunderous Autzen Stadium in Eugene, to the serene beauty of California's Memorial Stadium, the facilities and fans of the Pac-10 are almost as endearing as the teams themselves.

The history of each stadium in the Pac Ten Conference has its own unique qualities and beginnings, which are unlike any other.

ARIZONA

Arizona Stadium (1928), Tucson, Arizona

Set in Tucson with majestic views of the Santa Catalina Mountains, is Arizona Stadium. It was built in 1928 with an original capacity of just 7,000 seats. Stadium renovations and expansions in 1938, '47, '50, '65, '76, and '88 have raised capacity to its current level. Arizona played its first home game, October 12, 1929 against California Tech, winning 35-0.

Due to the incredible heat of Tucson, the Wildcats have chosen to play most of their home games at night. The first night game played was September 25, 1931 against San Diego State.

Both the east and west stands of the facility hold the most seats, with every seat offering an unobstructed view of the entire field. Most seats offer the luxury of seeing the Santa Catalina Mountains, the University of Arizona campus, and the city of Tucson. Arizona Stadium has updated concession and restroom facilities, as well as an enormous 4-tier press box, luxury suites, a gargantuan scoreboard, an updated sound system, as well as spacious locker rooms. Interestingly enough, Arizona Stadium also houses a telescope mirror laboratory under the eastern grandstands.

Wildcat fans have always supported their football teams, filling the stands on numerous occasions. October 22, 1994, 58,817 spectators witnessed Arizona beat UCLA 34-24. The 1998 season also brought packed houses to Arizona Stadium and the fans were treated to a 12-1 record.

NICKNAME:	Wildcats
MASCOT:	Wilbur
PLAYING SURFACE:	Grass
SEATING CAPACITY:	56,500
CURRENT HEAD COACH:	John Mackovic

NOTABLE PLAYERS/COACHES: Players: Chuck Cecil, Rob Waldrop, Teddy Bruschi, Chris McAlister. **Coaches:** J.F. "Pop" McKale, Darrell Mudra, Larry Smith, Dick Tomey, John Mackovic.

Photographs courtesy of University of Arizona Media Relations

Photographs courtesy of Arizona State University

ARIZONA STATE

Sun Devil Stadium (1958), Tempe, Arizona

Sun Devil Stadium/Frank Kush Field is the nation's only campus-owned facility, which houses an NFL team. It is also the largest on-campus stadium in the Pac-10. The stadium is a gorgeous work of architecture constructed into the Tempe Butte Mountain Range in 1958. The field is named in honor of legendary former head coach Frank Kush, who guided the Sun Devils in the 1960's and '70's.

On October 4, 1958 the Sun Devils played their first game in their new home against West Texas State, registering a 16-13 victory.

Original capacity was 30,000 seats. Upgrades have produced more seating and stadium amenities including: a gorgeous press box, luxury suites, skyboxes, the Intercollegiate Athletic Complex, and a jumbo scoreboard.

The facility hosts the NFL's Arizona Cardinals' home games and the annual Tostitos Fiesta Bowl. It has hosted a Super Bowl, as well as two college football National Championship games.

The Sun Devils have consistently led or been near the top of, Pac-10 annual attendance charts. Six times in the mid '80s they were tops. The Devils have played in front of 70,000+ fans at home, including the 1989 game versus rival Arizona, when, a then record 74,926 spectators crowded the stadium. During the 1996 season the Devils played in front of sell-out crowds consistently as they made their way to the Rose Bowl.

NICKNAME:	Sun Devils
MASCOT:	Sparky
PLAYING SURFACE:	Grass
SEATING CAPACITY:	73,656
CURRENT HEAD COACH:	Dirk Koetter

NOTABLE PLAYERS/COACHES: **Players:** Danny White, Mike Haynes, Mark Malone, Jake Plummer. **Coaches:** Millard "Dixie" Howell, Dan Devine, Frank Kush, John Cooper.

CALIFORNIA

Memorial Stadium (1923), Berkeley, California

The University of California's Memorial Stadium is one of college football's oldest facilities. Named in honor of all who fought in World War I, it opened the 1923 season as Cal grabbed its first win November 24, against hated rival Stanford. Designed in the early 1920's by John Galen Howard, G.F. Buckingham, and E.F. Carpenter, three world-noted architects, Memorial Stadium was patterned after the Roman Coliseum.

There are few places in all of college football that offer spectators such breathtaking scenery. Set in Strawberry Canyon, it boasts gorgeous views of the San Francisco skyline, as well as the Bay and Golden Gate Bridges.

Sellouts are the norm. On twenty-five different occasions, Memorial Stadium has packed in more than 80,000 spectators. One of the largest crowd totaled 83,000, as Cal hosted Navy September 27, 1947.

Memorial Stadium has garnered attention recently because it is built on the Hayward Fault and will have to undergo a multi-million dollar renovation process.

NICKNAME: Golden Bears
MASCOT: Oski Bear
PLAYING SURFACE: Grass
SEATING CAPACITY: 75,028
CURRENT HEAD COACH: Jeff Tedford
NOTABLE PLAYERS/COACHES: **Players:** Harold "Brick" Muller, Jackie Jensen, Hardy Nickerson, Regan Upshaw, Chidi Ahanotu. **Coaches:** Andy Smith, Lynn "Pappy" Waldorf, Bruce Snyder, Steve Mariucci.

Photo credit: John Guistina

Photo credit: Otto Greule Jr./Allsport

OREGON

Autzen Stadium (1967), Eugene, Oregon

Constructed in time for the 1967 season, Autzen Stadium/Rich Brooks Field is one of only a few West Coast stadiums which can compare favorably with the University of Washington's Husky Stadium in sheer crowd noise. Constructed near the Willamette River just north of its campus, it is named after Thomas J. Autzen—philanthropist and founder of the Autzen foundation. The field is named for former head football coach Rich Brooks, who led the Ducks for 18 seasons.

Built for approximately 2.5 million dollars, Autzen Stadium was constructed on 90 acres. Because there is no track inside the stadium, the seats were built just thirty feet off the sidelines. They are also elevated six feet high at the 50-yard line on both sides of the field with alternating shades of green every five yards.

The University of Oregon went on two different impressive home winning streaks. From 1989-'91, the Ducks had a 10-game winning streak, which has only been surpassed by their recent 20-game streak entering the 2001 season.

One of the biggest crowds to attend a game took place October 17, 1992, as Oregon hosted the defending co-national champion, Washington Huskies, in front of 47,612.

NICKNAME: Ducks
MASCOT: Donald Duck
PLAYING SURFACE: Artificial Turf
SEATING CAPACITY: 41,698
CURRENT HEAD COACH: Mike Bellotti
NOTABLE PLAYERS/COACHES: Players: Norm Van Brocklin, Mel Renfro, Dan Fouts, Joey Harrington. **Coaches:** Hugo Bezdek, Charles "Shy" Huntington, Len Casanova, Rich Brooks, Mike Bellotti.

OREGON STATE

Reser Stadium (1953), Corvallis, Oregon

Over the past few seasons, the Oregon State football program has been elevated to the top of the Pac-10. Coach Dennis Erickson has brought an exciting type of football, which should cement the Beavers as a conference challenger for years to come. Similarly, Reser Stadium, home of Beaver football, is one of the best facilities in the conference. Formerly known as Parker Stadium, Reser was built in 1958 with an original capacity of 28,000 seats. The stadium was renamed recently in honor of the Reser family, who are OSU graduates and generous donators to the university.

A number of stadium upgrades have enhanced the durability of Reser Stadium. The stadium boasts a 200-foot overhang, which keeps some spectators dry from the testy Northwest weather.

The most noticeable aspect of the stadium is the multi-million dollar Valley Football Center, which is situated at the north end zone. The Center is an impressive, tri-story complex that is home to a huge weight room and training area. The Tommy Prothro Locker Room, along with both the home and visiting locker rooms, reside in the complex. The first floor also houses the 1962 Heisman Trophy won by Terry Baker.

NICKNAME: Beavers
MASCOT: Benny Beaver
PLAYING SURFACE: Artificial Turf
SEATING CAPACITY: 35,362
CURRENT HEAD COACH: Dennis Erickson
NOTABLE PLAYERS/COACHES: **Players:** Terry Baker, Dave Marlette, Jonathan Smith, Ken Simonton. **Coaches:** Tommy Prothro, Dee Androse, Dennis Erickson.

Photo credit: Barry Schwarz/OSU Athletics

Top: USC Sports Information

Photo credit: Associated Press, AP

SOUTHERN CALIFORNIA
Los Angeles Memorial Coliseum (1923), Los Angeles, California

No school can boast more football tradition in the West than Southern California. In the same manner, no stadium has more history or tradition than the Los Angeles Memorial Coliseum. It has hosted almost every conceivable sporting and entertainment event. Built in time for the 1923 football season, the USC football program has been its longest and presently only tenant.

The first game played in the Coliseum was October 6, 1923, as USC beat Pomona College 23-7. Since that day the Coliseum has hosted two different Olympiads (the 1932 and '84), the UCLA Bruin football team (before their permanent move to the Rose Bowl), the NFL's Raiders and Rams, and MLB's Los Angeles Dodgers. It has housed many track and field competitions as well as motor cross events and concerts.

Memorial Coliseum boasts a permanent lighting system, updated locker and restroom facilities, an upgraded and luxurious press box, as well as a paramedic area and police substation. The Coliseum has a seating capacity of around 94,000 seats, but due to recent rearrangements, home games for USC generally do not draw more than 68,000. On many occasions, before the capacity scaled down, they routinely played in front of 95,000 fans, sometimes exceeding 100,000. Most of those games were against hated cross-town rival UCLA.

Southern California has had tremendous success in the Coliseum, winning eight National Championship titles.

NICKNAME:	Trojans
MASCOT:	Tommy Trojan
PLAYING SURFACE:	Grass
SEATING CAPACITY:	94,000
CURRENT HEAD COACH:	Pete Carroll

NOTABLE PLAYERS/COACHES: Players: John Wayne, Mike Garrett, O.J. Simpson, Pat Haden, Charles White, Anthony Munoz, Ronnie Lott, Marcus Allen, Bruce Mathews, (too many superstars to list). **Coaches:** Howard Jones, John McKay, John Robinson.

STANFORD

Stanford Stadium (1921), Stanford, California

The 85,500-seat Stanford Stadium was built in 1921 with an original capacity of 60,000 seats. It has hosted Stanford Cardinal football, track and field teams, the 1985 Super Bowl, the 1994 World Cup Soccer Tournament, as well as the annual East-West Shrine Game. The approximate cost of construction was $200,000.

The first game played in the newly constructed stadium was against bitter rival California, November 19, 1921. Though Stanford fell to the eventual Rose Bowl Champions that day, they were able to score the first touchdown.

Stanford Stadium is a huge and historical facility, and boasts newly remodeled aluminum seating, updated and spacious locker rooms, official's locker rooms, as well as an impressive press box.

One of the biggest crowds to ever see a Stanford football game at home took place November 16, 1935, as Stanford beat California 13-0 in front of, a record 94,000 spectators. Stanford draws huge crowds to every game, including against football powers USC, Notre Dame, Washington, and the University of Texas.

NICKNAME:	Cardinal
MASCOT:	The Tree
PLAYING SURFACE:	Grass
SEATING CAPACITY:	85,500
CURRENT HEAD COACH:	Buddy Teevens

NOTABLE PLAYERS/COACHES: **Players:** Ernie Nevers, Jim Plunkett, John Elway, John Lynch. **Coaches:** Glenn "Pop" Warner, Clark Shaugnessy, Bill Walsh, Dennis Green, Tyrone Willingham.

Photo credit: David Gonzales

Photo credit:Donald Miralle/Allsport   Top: Associated Press, AP

UCLA

Rose Bowl (1922), Los Angeles, California

One of the most legendary and enduring sites in all of college football is the historic Rose Bowl, home to the UCLA Bruins. Built in 1922, the Rose Bowl is located in Pasadena, California.

The Rose Bowl has seated more than 100,000 spectators on different occasions. The largest crowd was 106,869 on January 1, 1973, when USC battled Ohio State in the Rose Bowl game. Original capacity in 1922 was an impressive 57,000 seats.

The Rose Bowl is home to the annual Rose Bowl football game and Major League Soccer's, Los Angeles Galaxy. It has also housed four Super Bowls, including men's and women's World Cup Soccer events.

The Bruins have called the Rose Bowl home since the 1982 season, where they have won 69% of their games. UCLA has played in a number of Rose Bowl games as well. One such notable game came on January 1, 1954, as UCLA played the University of Michigan in the first national color telecast shown on nationwide hookup.

The stadium has undergone a number of alteration and upgrades. It boasts comfortable chair-back seating, unobstructed views of the gorgeous field from every seat, brand new scoreboards with messaging capabilities, a relatively new lighting system, and a refurbished press box.

The Rose Bowl is a national landmark, which should be attended by any sports fan.

NICKNAME: Bruins
MASCOT: Joe Bruin
PLAYING SURFACE: Grass
SEATING CAPACITY: 94,000
CURRENT HEAD COACH: Bob Toledo
NOTABLE PLAYERS/COACHES: Players: Jackie Robinson, Bob Waterfield, Gary Beban, Ken Norton Jr., Troy Aikman. **Coaches:** Tommy Prothro, Dick Vermeil, Terry Donahue, Bob Toledo.

WASHINGTON

Husky Stadium (1920), Seattle, Washington

The University of Washington's Husky Stadium was built in six months and twenty days in 1920. The original capacity of this structural marvel was 30,000 seats.

Before construction began, members of the stadium committee were sent to the future stadium site for data collection purposes. Their findings concluded that a stadium with a 60,000+ capacity could be built, but only if a correct longitudinal axis was established. Members of the astronomical department were sent to calculate the angle of the sun's rays on a specific date to come up with a proper axis. As a result, when the stadium was finished, the sunlight was almost completely eliminated from the player's eyes. The location of the venue also allowed spectators scenic views of Lake Washington, Mount Rainier, and the Seattle skyline.

UW was the first major college football school in the nation to implement the use of artificial turf in 1968. The stadium is home to the Pac-10's nicest track, and also houses the Don James Reception Center.

Every year it is regarded by opposing teams and players as one of the most intimidating places to play. Sell-outs are the norm in Seattle. In 1995 the Huskies set a school season attendance record averaging over 74,000 per game including a then record 76,125 fans, which witnessed a battle between Washington and the Black Knights of Army.

NICKNAME:	Huskies
MASCOT:	Harry Husky
PLAYING SURFACE:	Artificial Turf
SEATING CAPACITY:	72,500
CURRENT HEAD COACH:	Rick Neuheisel

NOTABLE PLAYERS/COACHES: Players: Hugh McElhenny, Warren Moon, Steve Emtman. **Coaches:** Enoch Bagshaw, Ralph "Pest" Welch, Jim Owens, Don James.

Photo credit: Otto Greule Jr./Allsport

WASHINGTON STATE

Clarence D. Martin Stadium (1936), Pullman, Washington

Photographs courtesy of Washington State University

Clarence D. Martin Stadium has been home to the Washington State Cougar football team since 1936. Named in honor of a former governor of the state, Martin Stadium has endured much adversity, which includes 65 years of wear and tear, as well as a costly fire which destroyed the south stands in 1970.

The original WSU field was known as Soldier Field and was built in 1892, but by 1936, the Cougar football team needed an enlarged and updated facility. The current stadium was built of wood and boasted an adequate scoreboard and press box. Through the years it has undergone a number of changes that included the construction of new stands after the fire. In 1972, WSU witnessed the implementation of artificial turf.

Crowds pack Martin Stadium for every Cougar home game. Record 40,000 spectators have been present on a number of occasions when Washington State host UCLA and in-state rival Washington.

NICKNAME: Cougars
MASCOT: Butch the Cougar
PLAYING SURFACE: Artificial Turf
SEATING CAPACITY: 37,600
CURRENT HEAD COACH: Mike Price
NOTABLE PLAYERS/COACHES: Players: Turk Edwards, Mel Hein, Drew Bledsoe, Ryan Leaf. **Coaches:** Bill "Lone Star" Dietz, Orin "Babe" Hollingbery, Dennis Erickson, Mike Price.

East Division
FLORIDA

GEORGIA

KENTUCKY

SOUTH CAROLINA

TENNESSEE

VANDERBILT

West Division
ALABAMA

ARKANSAS

AUBURN

LOUISIANA STATE

MISSISSIPPI

MISSISSIPPI STATE

Courtesy of the University of Georgia

THE S.E.C.
(SOUTHEASTERN CONFERENCE)

Built on toughness, tradition, and history, the Southeastern Conference is arguably the roughest, toughest, and most exciting league in the nation. Eight of the twelve schools which make-up the conference have won a form of college football's National Championship at least once in their school's history. From top to bottom there isn't another league which is as hotly and closely contested as the talent rich Southeastern Conference.

All the SEC schools play in magnificent stadiums, which are as scenic, beautiful, and electric, as they are monstrous. Each school spares no expense in making their facility as good or better than everyone else's. Spectator numbers in the Southeastern Conference are second only to the Big 10 in total attendance each year, and average attendance per game.

The history and tradition, which is imbedded in each of these SEC stadiums is uncommonly unique. Created by schools such as Alabama, Georgia, and Tennessee, elevated by players such as Don Hutson, Frank Sinkwich, Billy Cannon, Pat Sullivan, and Herschel Walker, and formed by coaches like Vince Dooley, Ralph "Shug" Jordan, and Paul "Bear" Bryant, the Southeastern Conference and its facilities were and are among college football's best.

From Georgia's hedges in Sanford Stadium, to Louisiana State's thunderous Tiger Stadium, SEC venues are sites to behold.

FLORIDA

Ben Hill Griffin Stadium (1930), Gainesville, Florida

Dedicated November 8, 1930, against the University of Alabama, Ben Hill Griffin Jr. Stadium is another in a long line of gorgeously constructed and magnificent Southeastern Conference facilities. The 83,000-seat home of the Gators comes complete with close to fifty skyboxes, 6,500 chair back seats, a contemporary athletic training center, as well as a gigantic press box. The stadium is also home to one of the most well-lighted facilities in the south and arguably, the best playing surface in the nation.

Known as "The Swamp", Florida Field in Ben Hill Griffin Stadium is loud and down-right intimidating for opposing teams. This facility consistently packs in more spectators than the registered capacity, and has been home to some of the biggest crowds in Gator history. One of the largest gatherings at Florida Field came against rival Florida State, November 25, 1995, when 85,711 spectators witnessed a Gator victory.

Named in honor of Ben Hill Griffin Jr., a long-time Gator fan and financial contributor, "The Swamp" is uniquely designed to centralize noise.

Since the early 1990's, the Gators have enjoyed playing in front of close to 85,000 people for every home game. These figures put the University of Florida near the top of the annual average attendance statistics.

NICKNAME:	Gators
MASCOT:	Albert
PLAYING SURFACE:	Grass
SEATING CAPACITY:	83,000
CURRENT HEAD COACH:	Ron Zook

NOTABLE PLAYERS/COACHES: Players: Steve Spurrier, Wes Chandler, Jack Youngblood, Emmitt Smith, Danny Wuerffel, Rex Grossman. **Coaches:** Charley Pell, Steve Spurrier.

Photo credit: University of Florida News and Public Affairs

Courtesy of the University of Georgia

GEORGIA

Sanford Stadium (1929), Athens, Georgia

Sanford Stadium is one of the most scenic and exciting places to watch a college football game. Set in the heart of the Georgia campus, Sanford Stadium epitomizes everything that college football should be. The facility was built in 1929 at a cost of $360,000, and was named in honor of Dr. Steadman Vincent Sanford. Original capacity was an impressive 30,000.

The upgrades done to the stadium over the years has elevated it to one of the best football facilities in the entire nation. The comfortable, yet intense and electric atmosphere, which the stadium exudes, can be attributed to the design of the structure, and to the fans.

Sanford is home to a luxurious press box, numerous skyboxes, a huge contemporary scoreboard, and updated concession facilities. The Bulldogs also play on a beautiful grass surface, which is surrounded by the world's most famous hedges. Comfortable seating allows for unobstructed views of the entire field.

One of the most remarkable aspects of the facility is the UGA tomb, which is home to the deceased bulldog mascots. They are at rest within the walls near the north end zone.

The University of Georgia boasts a rich and storied history, and the stadium has been a major part of it since it opened more than 70 years ago. The Georgia fans consistently show their support for their "Dawgs" year in and year out, averaging close to 85,000 per game.

NICKNAME: Bulldogs
MASCOT: UGA VI
PLAYING SURFACE: Grass
SEATING CAPACITY: 86,117
CURRENT HEAD COACH: Mark Richt
NOTABLE PLAYERS/COACHES: Players: Frank Sinkwich, Charlie Trippi, Fran Tarkenton, Jake Scott, Herschel Walker, Terrell Davis. **Coaches:** Glenn "Pop" Warner, Wally Butts, Vince Dooley.

KENTUCKY

Commonwealth Stadium (1973), Lexington, Kentucky

Commonwealth Stadium is simply a gorgeous facility. Set on the University of Kentucky campus, it was built upon a patch of land, which once housed the UK Experimental Station Farm. Since it opened September 15, 1973, Commonwealth Stadium has been a magnificent fixture, for both the University of Kentucky football program, and the UK campus. Kentucky opened the venue by defeating Virginia Tech 31-26.

There is no denying the rich basketball tradition of UK, but the school is more than a basketball power. The facility attests to the commitment the school has shown towards the football program. The Wildcat home is complete with a spacious press box, permanent lighting, as well as a mammoth scoreboard and message center.

Since opening, the stadium has averaged over 55,000 spectators per game. One of Commonwealth's largest attended games took place in 1994 against hated rival Louisville, when 59,162 fans packed in to to watch the Wildcats defeat the Cardinals 20-14. The fans have proven to be outstanding and loyal college football enthusiasts, while Commonwealth Stadium has become a jewel in the university's eyes.

NICKNAME: Wildcats
MASCOT: Wildcat & Scratch
PLAYING SURFACE: Grass
SEATING CAPACITY: 65,000
CURRENT HEAD COACH: Guy Morriss
NOTABLE PLAYERS/COACHES: **Players:** George Blanda, Babe Parilli, Lou Michaels, Tim Couch. **Coaches:** Paul "Bear" Bryant, Jerry Claiborne.

Top: Courtesy of University of Kentucky

Photo credit: ©Breck Smither

Top: Courtesy of University of South Carolina Sports Information

Photo credit: Jason Wolfe

SOUTH CAROLINA

Williams-Brice Stadium (1934), Columbia, South Carolina

Built in 1934, Williams-Brice Stadium offers players and spectators all the comforts that one would expect in a Southeastern Conference facility. The stadium is named in honor of Martha Williams Brice, who bequeathed a sum of no less than one million dollars to the University of South Carolina, which was used to renovate the Gamecock football facility.

The venue is one of the largest college football facilities in the south, and is home to a number of contemporary amenities, which include: permanent lighting, spacious locker rooms, an updated press box, as well as a number of luxury suites. Also found in the facility are many comfortable chairback seats and accommodations for the handicapped which include telecommunication devices for the deaf.

Due to the resurgence of the football program in the last couple of years, South Carolina has made a habit of playing in front of crowds which reach, or surpass, stadium capacity. One of the largest attended games took place September 2001, when they hosted Alabama in front of 85,000+ frenzied fans.

Since the arrival of Head Coach Lou Holtz and his staff, the Gamecock's program has aggressively moved towards the top of the national rankings. Coach Holtz's guidance combined with the impressive Williams-Brice Stadium, should attract the best talent the Southeast has to offer.

NICKNAME:	Gamecocks
MASCOT:	Cocky
PLAYING SURFACE:	Grass
SEATING CAPACITY:	82,250
CURRENT HEAD COACH:	Lou Holtz

NOTABLE PLAYERS/COACHES: Players: George Rogers, Sterling Sharpe, Duce Staley, John Abraham. **Coaches:** Paul Dietzel, Jim Carlen, Joe Morrison, Lou Holtz.

TENNESSEE

Neyland Stadium/Shields-Watkins Field (1921),
Knoxville, Tennessee

General Robert R. Neyland Stadium is the South's biggest college football venue. Set on the banks of the Tennessee River in gorgeous Knoxville, it is easily accessible by car or boat.

In 1919, Col. W.S. Fields, a University of Tennessee trustee and president of City National Bank, started the drive to build a facility that would showcase Volunteer football. By 1921, a 3,200-seat site had been erected.

A few years later General Robert Neyland took over as the head coach, and immediately brought the Volunteers to national prominence. Dedication of Neyland Stadium took place October 20, 1962, against rival Alabama.

Since 1921, the stadium has undergone close to fifteen renovations, which have helped elevate capacity to its current level.

At home, the Volunteers have been nearly unbeatable. In their 80+ years, Tennessee has registered 70 winning seasons, many in which they went undefeated. The school can also boast a 30-game consecutive home winning streak, which started December 8, 1928, against Florida, and ended October 21, 1933, against Alabama.

From 1950-'95, more than 65,000 people on average have attended each home game. Due to recent expansions, average home attendance is over 100,000 per contest.

NICKNAME: Volunteers
MASCOT: Smokey VIII & The Volunteer
PLAYING SURFACE: Grass
SEATING CAPACITY: 104,079
CURRENT HEAD COACH: Phillip Fulmer
NOTABLE PLAYERS/COACHES: **Players:** Players: Bobby Dodd, Doug Atkins, Johnny Majors, Reggie White, Peyton Manning, Tee Martin, John Henderson. **Coaches:** General Robert Neyland, Johnny Majors, Phillip Fulmer.

Courtesy of The Photography Center University of Tennessee

VANDERBILT

Vanderbilt Stadium (1922), Nashville, Tennessee

The site where Vanderbilt Stadium now sits was known as Dr. William Dudley Field until 1980. Constructed in 1922 and named for the Dean of the Vanderbilt Medical College, Dudley Field served as the Commodores home until the 1981 season. Dedicated October 14, 1922 against the University of Michigan, the field held the dubious distinction of being the first football-only facility built in the South. Original capacity sat at an impressive 22,000.

In just nine short months beginning in December 1980, the field was completely demolished and reconstructed. Vanderbilt Stadium was dedicated September 1981, in a game versus heavily-favored Maryland. That day the Commodores upset the Terrapins 23-17, which marked the start of a new beginning for Vanderbilt football.

The facility comes complete with a 17,000 square-foot press box, numerous luxury box and theatre seats, ten restrooms, over a half-dozen concession stands, as well as a couple of first aid stations. Both the visiting and home locker rooms at the stadium are over 10,000 square feet in size.

Though the Commodores have not enjoyed the winning tradition that other SEC schools have, the fans still support their teams. Home crowds of over 35,000 fans are the norm for the Vanderbilt program.

NICKNAME:	Commodores
MASCOT:	Mr. Commodore
PLAYING SURFACE:	Grass
SEATING CAPACITY:	41,600
CURRENT HEAD COACH:	Bobby Johnson

NOTABLE PLAYERS/COACHES: **Players:** Josh Cody, Lynn Bomar, Carl Hinkle. **Coaches:** Art Guepe, Steve Sloan.

ALABAMA

Bryant-Denny Stadium (1929), Tuscaloosa, Alabama

Possibly the greatest power in the history of college football, the University of Alabama has always been a mark of excellence. The Crimson Tide play their home games in two different facilities: Bryant-Denny Stadium, which sits on the Alabama campus in Tuscaloosa, and Legion Field in Birmingham.

Dedicated October 5, 1929, against Ole Miss, 11,000 fans showed up in the 12,072-seat facility to watch Alabama win 22-7. The stadium is named in honor of legendary Head Coach Paul "Bear" Bryant and former university president George H. Denny.

Alabama's first game in Legion Field was October 8, 1927, when they battled Louisiana State University. Since that game, the Crimson Tide has enjoyed an outstanding record in Birmingham, winning close to 73% of their games. Due to the renovations at Bryant-Denny Stadium in 1988, Alabama played all of their home games that season at Legion Field.

Both Bryant-Denny Stadium and Legion Field offer the Crimson Tide a home field advantage which few schools can identify with. Of note, Bryant's winning record at Bryant-Denny stood at 97.3%. Losing only two games in Tuscaloosa, the "Bear" went 72-2 over twenty-five seasons, which included a 57-consecutive game home winning streak that stemmed from October 1963 to November 1982.

NICKNAME: Crimson Tide
MASCOT: Big Al
PLAYING SURFACE: Grass
SEATING CAPACITY: 83,818
CURRENT HEAD COACH: Dennis Franchione
NOTABLE PLAYERS/COACHES: Players: Don Hutson, Bart Starr, Lee Roy Jordan, Joe Namath, Ken Stabler, John Hannah, Cornelius Bennett, Derrick Thomas. **Coaches:** Wallace Wade, Frank Thomas, Paul "Bear" Bryant, Gene Stallings.

Photo credit: Associated Press, AP

Photographs courtesy of University of Arkansas Sports Information Office

ARKANSAS

Razorback Stadium (1938), Fayetteville, Arkansas

Much like SEC-foe Alabama, the University of Arkansas also plays their home games at two beautiful facilities. Both Razorback Stadium, which is Arkansas' primary home, and War Memorial Stadium, in Little Rock, have been a major part of Arkansas' home success for over 50 years.

Set on the Arkansas campus, Razorback Stadium was a 13,500-seat architectural marvel when it opened in 1938. The stadium was part of the Government's Works Progress Administration (WPA) project in the late 1930's, and was dedicated October 8, 1938, against the Baylor Bears.

The stadium is one of the most fan-friendly environments in the south. An upgraded press box, enlarged locker rooms, and a huge "Smartvision Led" video screen, dubbed as the largest video board at any sports venue in the world, have kept Razorback Stadium competitive with the rest of the SEC.

Like Razorback Stadium, War Memorial Stadium offers spectators and players every amenity available for comfort. Dedicated in 1948, War Memorial holds well over 50,000 fans and is also home to one of the best media press boxes in the entire nation. The first Arkansas football game played in the facility was September 18, 1948, against Abilene Christian University. One of the biggest crowds to watch a game at the War, took place September 19, 1992, when Alabama came to town. Though Alabama came away with the win, and the eventual National Championship, 60,000 Arkansas fans showed their support by packing into Memorial Stadium.

NICKNAME: Razorbacks
MASCOT: Big Red
PLAYING SURFACE: Grass
SEATING CAPACITY: 72,000
CURRENT HEAD COACH: Houston Nutt
NOTABLE PLAYERS/COACHES: **Players:** Lance Alworth, Loyd Phillips, Barry Foster. **Coaches:** Frank Broyles, Lou Holtz, Houston Nutt.

AUBURN

Jordan-Hare Stadium (1939), Auburn, Alabama

Mammoth Jordan-Hare Stadium is home to the University of Auburn football team. Dedicated November 30, 1939, against the University of Florida, then known as Auburn Stadium, it originally had a seating capacity of 7,500. The facility has undergone a number of facelifts, which have helped make Jordan-Hare, Alabama's fifth largest city during Tiger home football games.

Renovations, which started in 1949, and continued through the Shug Jordan and Pat Dye regimes, have elevated Jordan-Hare to the upper-echelon of SEC football venues. The facility boasts an updated press box, luxury suites, refurbished locker rooms, and a gorgeous playing field. As is the custom of every SEC facility, the home for Auburn football is deafening, and the fans are always electric.

Named in honor of Auburn's legendary head coach Ralph "Shug" Jordan and former alumnus, and president of the Auburn Faculty Athletic Committee, Clifford Hare, the stadium consistently draws over 80,000 fans per game in a town which has a weekday population of just 35,000 people.

One of the most memorable Auburn home games came at the expense of hated-rival Alabama. December 2, 1989, the number two ranked, and unbeaten, Crimson Tide, visited Jordan-Hare Stadium leaving a 30-20 loser. That game was played in front of a record crowd 85,319 spectators.

NICKNAME: Tigers or War Eagles
MASCOT: Aubie & Tiger (the Golden Eagle)
PLAYING SURFACE: Grass
SEATING CAPACITY: 85,612
CURRENT HEAD COACH: Tommy Tuberville
NOTABLE PLAYERS/COACHES: **Players:** Pat Sullivan, William Andrews, Joe Cribbs, James Brooks, Bo Jackson, Kevin Greene. **Coaches:** Ralph "Shug" Jordan, Pat Dye.

Courtesy of Auburn University

LOUISIANA STATE
Tiger Stadium (1924), Baton Rouge, Louisiana

Photographs courtesy of Louisiana State University

Tiger Stadium is simply the most deafening and intimidating place to play for opposing teams anywhere in the nation. When the sun goes down in Baton Rouge, the atmosphere turns explosive. Tiger Stadium is also known as "Death Valley" and for good reason – many great college football teams have traveled to Baton Rouge with thoughts of a National Championship only to have those aspirations dashed.

The Tigers have played in the facility since 1924. Due to the fact that most of the LSU home football games take place at night, much of the attention centers on the stadium atmosphere in the evening. But make no mistake, the fans are just as enthusiastic during the day, and the LSU football teams are just as good.

Due to the many upgrades, which have enhanced the seating capacity, the stadium has thus been reconfigured to bring spectators closer to the playing field. This, of course, makes an already electric situation almost unbearable for visiting squads.

Year in and year out people pack Tiger Stadium regardless of the success of the team. The facility has averaged over 70,000 spectators per game, thus making Tiger fans some of the most loyal the nation has to offer.

NICKNAME:	Tigers
MASCOT:	Mike
PLAYING SURFACE:	Grass
SEATING CAPACITY:	91,600
CURRENT HEAD COACH:	Nick Saban

NOTABLE PLAYERS/COACHES: Players: Billy Cannon, Jim Taylor, Bert Jones. **Coaches:** Bernie Moore, Paul Dietzel, Charlie McClendon, Nick Saban.

MISSISSIPPI (Ole Miss)

Vaught-Hemingway Stadium (1915), Oxford, Mississippi

Nestled gently on the Ole Miss campus in Oxford, sits the historic, and well-designed, Vaught-Hemingway Stadium. Few campuses are as spectacular to the eye as the University of Mississippi, and few facilities offer spectators such breathtaking views like Vaught-Hemingway. The facility is named in honor of the former Professor of Law at Ole Miss and Chairman of the Committee on Athletics, Judge William Hemingway and legendary head football coach John Vaught.

Not only is it one of the nation's prettiest facilities, it is also one of the oldest. Construction on the site where the stadium now stands first took place by Ole Miss students in 1915.

One of the largest crowds to ever witness a game in Vaught-Hemingway took place in 1995 against Alabama when 44,312 fans watched the Rebels battle the Crimson Tide. Although capacity has recently been enlarged, the stadium is packed consistently.

The facility has the odd distinction of having the nation's longest press box, which stretches 80 yards. Parking at Ole Miss is very conducive to tailgating, which helps make Ole Miss home football games a great game-day experience.

NICKNAME: Rebels
MASCOT: Colonel Rebel
PLAYING SURFACE: Grass
SEATING CAPACITY: 50,577
CURRENT HEAD COACH: David Cutcliffe
NOTABLE PLAYERS/COACHES: **Players:** Charlie Conerly, Charlie Flowers, Archie Manning, Eli Manning. **Coaches:** John Vaught, Billy Brewer, David Cutcliffe.

Courtesy of the University of Mississippi

Photographs courtesy of Mississippi State

MISSISSIPPI STATE

Scott Field (1914), Mississippi State, Mississippi

Since Jackie Sherrill took over as head football coach at Mississippi State University, the Bulldogs have consistently challenged conference foes for top billing in the SEC Western Division. In much the same way, Davis Wade Stadium/Scott Field, has also undergone a number of recent renovations, which have made the facility the beautiful place it is today.

Built in 1914, Davis Wade Stadium/Scott Field is named for two very distinguished and important gentlemen who helped the Mississippi State football program take shape. Davis Wade has generously donated a great deal of money to further the expansion of Scott Field, which will raise seating capacity from 40,676, to 52,000+. Don Magruder Scott, the field's namesake, was one of Mississippi State's first great college football players and track stars. Scott went on to become an Olympic sprinter.

The stadium boasts all the amenities to be expected of an SEC school, including; the Turman Fieldhouse, home to the MSU Heritage Room, along with offices for Alumni gatherings.

Since the early 1990's, the MSU faithful have consistently packed the stadium to near capacity. With the upgrades and additions to Wade Stadium nearly finished, the facility should be the jewel of the MSU campus.

NICKNAME: Bulldogs
MASCOT: Bully
PLAYING SURFACE: Grass
SEATING CAPACITY: 52,000+
CURRENT HEAD COACH: Jackie Sherrill
NOTABLE PLAYERS/COACHES: **Players:** Don Scott, Eric Moulds, Greg Favors, Fred Smoot. **Coaches:** Emory Bellard, Jackie Sherrill.

ARKANSAS STATE

IDAHO

LOUISIANA-LAFAYETTE

LOUISIANA-MONROE

MIDDLE TENNESSEE STATE

NEW MEXICO STATE

NORTH TEXAS

Photo credit: Jason Wolfe

SUN BELT CONFERENCE

The newly formed Sun Belt Conference consist of up and coming hard-nosed football programs which are spread throughout the country. Although only seven schools comprise the Sun Belt, it is a certainty that this conference will be one of the most exciting leagues in the nation.

Some of the schools are relatively new to Division 1-A, while others have been a staple on college football's top level for decades. The players and teams, which comprise the Sun Belt are very talented and the crowds are no less loyal than their bigger conference counterparts.

Although there are no 80,000-seat stadiums that reside in this conference, all the venues are fan friendly and historic in their own rite. Some may argue that these stadiums are just as scenic as those in any conference. From Indian Stadium on the Arkansas State University campus to Middle Tennessee State's Johnny "Red" Floyd Stadium, the facilities of the Sun Belt have as much pride in looks and comfort as any in the nation.

ARKANSAS STATE

Indian Stadium (1974), State University, Arkansas

Indian Stadium has been home to Arkansas State football since 1974. Within its friendly confines, Arkansas State teams have posted a winning record 60%. The Indians also had an impressive home winning streak of 17 games, which spanned from 1984-'87.

Original capacity was 16,343 seats when the facility opened September 28, 1974. The Indians first opponent was Louisiana Tech University. In ASU's second game, they defeated Eastern Michigan 14-7, for their inagural victory.

Though the campus is set in the tiny town of Jonesboro, Arkansas, the Indian fans have always done a wonderful job in supporting their teams. One of the largest crowds to witness a game took place October 26, 1991, when nearly 21,000 fans watched Arkansas State play Southwest Missouri State University. That same year an attendance record was set by the Indian faithful when Arkansas State averaged 17,454 spectators per game.

NICKNAME: Indians
MASCOT: Indian Family
PLAYING SURFACE: Grass
SEATING CAPACITY: 33,410
CURRENT HEAD COACH: Steve Roberts
NOTABLE PLAYERS/COACHES: Players: Cleo Lemon, Ray Brown, Kyle Richardson, Carlos Emmons.
Coaches: Ray Perkins.

Courtesy of Arkansas State University

Courtesy of University of Idaho Photo Services

IDAHO

William H. Kibbie/ASUI Activity Center (1975)
Moscow, Idaho

The William H. Kibbie Dome, a truly unique multi-purpose facility, was praised by the American Society of Engineers as "America's Outstanding Structural Engineering Achievement of 1976".

Named for Idaho alumnus William H. Kibbie, who graciously contributed monetarily to the project, the Kibbie Dome was built in three major segments, starting in 1971, and ending in 1982. Built mainly because of the fire which destroyed the old football facility in 1969, the Kibbie Dome is home to the Vandal Basketball and track teams, and their up-and-coming football team.

One of the largest crowds to ever see a game in the Kibbie Dome took place November 18, 1989, when the Vandals played cross-state rival Boise State, in front of 17,600 spectators.

The Kibbie Dome is also home to an immaculate training area for all university athletes, as well as spacious locker rooms for both home and visiting football teams. There are eight racquetball courts, a number of meeting rooms, a huge weight room, and many offices for staff personnel.

Idaho has close to a 72% winning record at home and show no signs of slowing down.

NICKNAME: Vandals
MASCOT: Joe Vandal
PLAYING SURFACE: Artificial Turf
SEATING CAPACITY: 16,000+
CURRENT HEAD COACH: Tom Cable
NOTABLE PLAYERS/COACHES: **Players:** Wayne Walker, John Friesz, Doug Nussmeier. **Coaches:** Chris Tormey, Tom Cable.

LOUISIANA-LAFAYETTE

Cajun Field (1971), Lafayette, Louisiana

The Ragin' Cajuns has always been a competitive Division 1-A football program. Cajun Field successfully opened September 25, 1971, when Louisiana-Lafayette beat Santa Clara University 21-0. Throughout the years, "The Swamp" has been a symbol of dominance for the Ragin' Cajun football program. Louisiana-Lafayette has been so good at home that major football powers such as Alabama and Texas A&M have accepted invitations to come to Lafayette.

Constructed in a bowl shape, Cajun Field is set two feet below sea level. As one may have guessed, drainage may be a huge problem for Cajun Field. A well-built drainage system along with high-powered pumps have alleviated any prospective problems. Cajun Field took on the nickname, "The Swamp", for a number of different reasons stemming from the landscape of the stadium itself to the fact that the National Wetlands Center is only a half-mile away.

Original capacity was only 26,500. Fan support and the success of Louisiana-Lafayette football teams, have allowed the University to expand seating. One of the biggest crowds to witness a game at Lafayette took place October 6, 1990, as 36,000 watched the Ragin' Cajuns battle superpower Alabama. Since its opening, Cajun Field has averaged close to 20,000 fans per game. In 1975, average attendance was over 25,000.

NICKNAME:	Ragin' Cajuns
MASCOT:	Cayenne
PLAYING SURFACE:	Grass
SEATING CAPACITY:	31,500
CURRENT HEAD COACH:	Rickey Bustle

NOTABLE PLAYERS/COACHES: Players: Brian Mitchell, Orlando Thomas, Brandon Stokley. **Coaches:** T.R. Mobley, Russ Faulkinberry, Nelson Stokley.

Courtesy of University of Louisiana-Lafayette

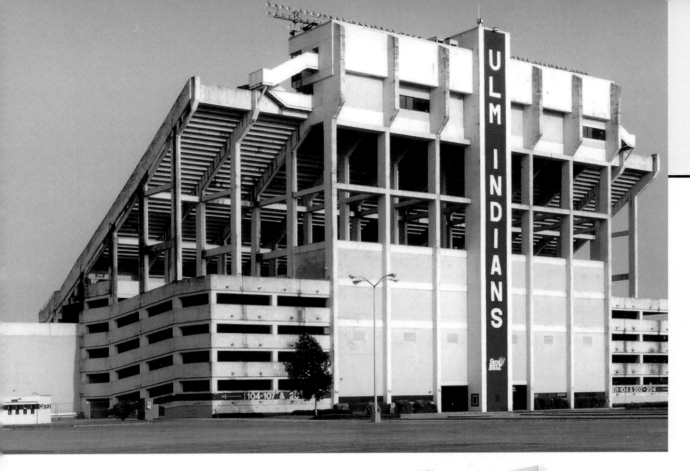

LOUISIANA-MONROE

Malone Stadium (1978), Monroe, Louisiana

Since 1978, Louisiana-Monroe has played their home football games at James L. Malone Stadium. The stadium opened for play September 16, 1978, as the Indians beat Arkansas State University 21-13. Named in honor of James L. Malone, one of Louisiana-Monroe's (then known as Northeast Louisiana University) most successful football coaches, it is another gorgeous Division 1-A football facility.

It is home to 3,000 chair back seats and 27,500 aluminum seats, making the venue one of the most comfortable spectator facilities in the conference. It also boasts a luxurious press box, a booster skybox, permanent lighting, and a magnificent 38,000 square-foot field house, which resides under the westside stands. The field house is home to dozens of offices and sports rooms, a sports medicine complex, and a turf room that is both a practice facility and weight room.

Since its opening, Malone Stadium and the Indian football teams have enjoyed an impressive and consistent display of fan loyalty. The Indians average nearly 18,000 fans per game, and have exceeded 23,000 spectators on a number of occasions. The Indians have an impressive home winning record of 70% while winning 95% of their home openers.

NICKNAME:	Indians
MASCOT:	Chief Brave Spirit
PLAYING SURFACE:	Grass
SEATING CAPACITY:	30,427
CURRENT HEAD COACH:	Bobby Keasler

NOTABLE PLAYERS/COACHES: Players: Stan Humphries, Jackie Harris, Vincent Brisby, Irving Spikes. **Coaches:** James L. Malone

Courtesy of University of Louisiana-Monroe

MIDDLE TENNESSEE STATE

Johnny "Red" Floyd Stadium (1933), Murfreesboro, Tennessee

The Blue Raiders play on one of the prettiest home fields in the entire nation. Floyd Stadium is a beautiful blend of creativity, color, and contemporary architecture. The only reason Johnny "Red" Floyd Stadium does not get any national notoriety is because it resides in the unpopular Sun Belt Conference.

Johnny "Red" Floyd was an extremely successful head coach for the Blue Raider football program during the mid-1930's. He coached MTSU during the 1917 season while a member of the Vanderbilt football squad. That year the Commodores did not play any games, allowing Coach Floyd to focus all his time and energy down in Murfreesboro.

Built originally in 1933, on what was known as Horace Jones Field, Johnny Floyd Stadium undertook a number of major renovations. In 1960 the seating capacity was raised to 10,000 seats. The largest home crowd to see a Blue Raiders game took place September 5, 1998, when the Blue Raiders hosted rival Tennessee State in front of 27,568 screaming fans.

This gorgeous facility is home to a number of luxury box seats, a huge press box area, a camera deck, as well as an impressive artificial turf-playing surface. The grandstands touch the sky vertically, which allows the crowd noise to stay inside the stadium.

Floyd Stadium is a gem that will hopefully help bring the Blue Raider football program into the national spotlight.

NICKNAME: Blue Raiders
MASCOT: Lightning
PLAYING SURFACE: Artificial Turf
SEATING CAPACITY: 30,788
CURRENT HEAD COACH: Andy McCollum
NOTABLE PLAYERS/COACHES: **Players:** Jimbo Pearson, Mike Caldwell, Jonathan Quinn, Marty Carter. **Coaches:** Johnny "Red" Floyd.

Courtesy of Middle Tennessee Media Relations

NEW MEXICO STATE

Aggie Memorial Stadium (1977), Las Cruces, New Mexico

Aggie Memorial Stadium is the proud home to the New Mexico State University Aggies. It is named in memory of the veterans of the Korean War and the Vietnam Conflict associated with the university. The stadium opened its gates in 1978, when New Mexico State beat rival UTEP 35-32 on dedication day. Aggie Memorial was built at a relatively low cost of four million dollars.

The complex is home to immaculate locker room facilities along with the impressive 13,500 sq. foot weight room, which would make any powerhouse programs envious.

The Aggie faithful are a major factor in the success of New Mexico State football. One of the largest crowds to see a game in Aggie Memorial took place in 1998 against UTEP, when 32,993 fans witnessed an Aggie 33-24 win.

Coach Tony Samuel's hard-fighting teams have been, and will continue to be, a serious threat at home.

NICKNAME: Aggies
MASCOT: Aggie the Cowboy
PLAYING SURFACE: Hybrid Bermuda Turf
SEATING CAPACITY: 30,343
CURRENT HEAD COACH: Tony Samuel
NOTABLE PLAYERS/COACHES: Players: Tim Engelhardt, Chris Barnes, Joey Dozier. **Coaches:** Jerry Hines, Warren Woodson.

NORTH TEXAS

Fouts Field (1951), Denton, Texas

The Mean Green, of North Texas, play their home football games in the spectacular Theron J. Fouts Field. Mr. Fouts was a unique and talented man who coached all of the North Texas sports at the university. In addition to being the head football coach and athletic director, Fouts created the track and field teams at North Texas, as well as directing the golf, and basketball programs.

Built in 1951 with an original capacity of 20,000 seats, Fouts Field has undergone a number of renovations. The major construction project that began in December of 1993 and ended in the summer of 1994, added an extra 10,500 seats. Outlining the artificial turf field is an all weather track and shot-put area. Fouts Field also is home to an impressive athletic complex, which houses a huge weight room and sports medicine facility.

Fouts Field is no stranger to large crowds. Prior to the mid-90's expansion, the Mean Green played a number of home games in front of 20,000+ spectators, which, at the time, surpassed stadium capacity. One of the largest pre-expansion crowds to witness a home game was October 6, 1990, as North Texas beat Southern Methodist University 14-7 in front of 22,750 spectators. Since the expansion, the Mean Green have played occasionally in front of more than 25,000 spectators.

NICKNAME: Mean Green/Eagles
MASCOT: Scrappy
PLAYING SURFACE: Artificial Turf
SEATING CAPACITY: 30,500
CURRENT HEAD COACH: Darrell Dickey
NOTABLE PLAYERS/COACHES: **Players:** "Mean" Joe Greene, Ja'Quay Wilburn. **Coaches:** Theron J. Fouts, Odus Mitchell, Hayden Fry.

Photo credit: North Texas Athletic Department:

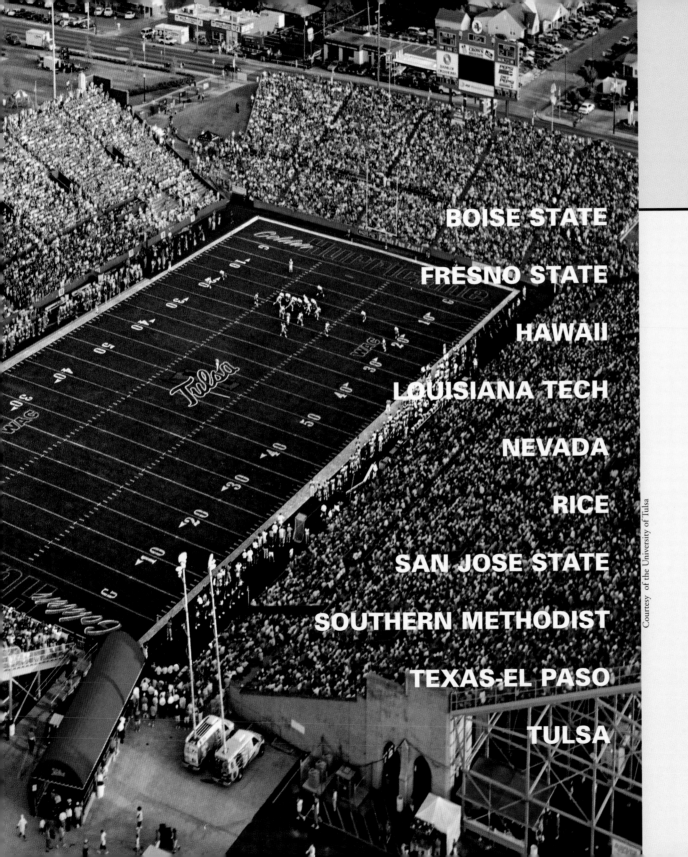

BOISE STATE

FRESNO STATE

HAWAII

LOUISIANA TECH

NEVADA

RICE

SAN JOSE STATE

SOUTHERN METHODIST

TEXAS-EL PASO

TULSA

Courtesy of the University of Tulsa

WESTERN ATHLETIC CONFERENCE

Five years ago, the landscape of the Western Athletic Conference was remarkably different than it is today. Almost every school which was a part of the WAC at that time, has now moved to the Mountain West Conference. Although match-ups like the BYU/San Diego State-type have relocated elsewhere, the WAC is still as eccentric as ever, and the teams are every bit as exciting.

As many of these football programs gain recognition, the stadiums in which their games are played will also become increasingly familiar. The WAC boasts some of college football's most electric and fan friendly facilities. These venues are gorgeous to look at, scenic in their locations, and produce some of the loudest atmospheres anywhere. From Nevada's Mackay Stadium to Hawaii's Aloha Stadium, the WAC facilities are as different from each other as the teams.

BOISE STATE

Bronco Stadium (1970), Boise, Idaho

The bright blue football field inside Bronco Stadium is its most recognizable characteristic. The gorgeous Bronco Stadium was built in 1970 at a cost of 2.2 million dollars. Original capacity for the facility was an impressive; 14,500 seats.

The stadium is much more than a facility that houses the nation's only blue playing field; it also is home to the state-of-the-art Allen Noble Hall of Fame Gallery, as well as the Larry and Marianne Williams Plaza. Both the Gallery and Plaza are incredibly spacious and house a number of meeting rooms and offices which serve every conceivable function. The Gallery hosts all the major Boise State athletic awards as well as plaques of former Bronco greats. The Williams Plaza has a massive kitchen, which supports the many alumni functions. The Gallery and Plaza Complex are located at the southwest corner of Bronco Stadium.

The fans that fill Bronco Stadium are as loud and electric as their Bronco team. On many occasions the Broncos have played in front of 25,000 rabid spectators. The jump from the Big West Conference to the ever-popular Western Athletic Conference will give the Bronco football teams, as well as the Boise State fans, many chances to showcase their abilities. The nation will soon see what the western part of the United States has known for some time, that Bronco Stadium is one of the nicest college football facilities anywhere.

NICKNAME: Broncos
MASCOT: Buster the Bronco
PLAYING SURFACE: Blue Artificial Turf
SEATING CAPACITY: 30,000
CURRENT HEAD COACH: Dan Hawkins
NOTABLE PLAYERS/COACHES: **Players:** Bart Hendricks, Bryan Johnson, Corey Nelson. **Coaches:** Pokey Allen, Houston Nutt, Dirk Koetter.

Courtesy of Fresno State

FRESNO STATE

Bulldog Stadium (1980), Fresno, California

Bulldog Stadium/Jim Sweeney Field is built below sea level, placing the field close to forty feet in the ground. It is a clean and comfortable facility, which boasts nearly 10,000 chair back seats, monstrous light standards, a luxurious press box, as well as close to 25 sky-suites. The field is named in honor of Jim Sweeney, the legendary former head coach who first brought the Bulldog program into the national spotlight in the mid-1980s.

It was built in 1980 at a cost of seven million dollars. The money generated for stadium construction came directly out of the pockets of the residents of the San Joaquin Valley. Original capacity of the new facility was 30,000 seats. It opened in style as the Bulldogs defeated Montana State University 21-14 November 15, 1980.

When one thinks of loyal football crowds, the Universities of Nebraska and Michigan come to mind. But some of the best fans in the entire nation frequent Fresno State games. Not only has Bulldog Stadium consistently sold out, in 2000 they averaged more fans than there were seats. During their 21 seasons in the facility, Fresno State has accumulated a remarkable winning record of over 80%.

With the talent that coach Pat Hill is bringing to Fresno along with the support of the fans, it seems that the Bulldogs are well on their way to be a constant national contender.

NICKNAME: Bulldogs
MASCOT: Time Out
PLAYING SURFACE: Grass
SEATING CAPACITY: 41,031
CURRENT HEAD COACH: Pat Hill
NOTABLE PLAYERS/COACHES: Players: Trent Dilfer, Lorenzo Neal, David Carr. **Coaches:** Alvin "Pix" Pierson, Cecil Coleman, Jim Sweeney, Pat Hill.

HAWAII

Aloha Stadium (1975), Honolulu, Hawaii

Aloha Stadium is one of the most diverse stadiums in all of college football. The home for the University of Hawaii Rainbow Warrior football team, Aloha Stadium also hosts the annual NFL Pro Bowl, college football's Aloha and Hula Bowls, along with various concerts, soccer matches, and the weekend Hawaiian flea market. Due to moveable grandstands, Aloha Stadium can be made into a triangle shape for concerts, a diamond for baseball games, and, of course, an oval for the traditional football games that are played there.

University of Hawaii first played in Aloha Stadium September 13, 1975, before 32,247 screaming fans. Although they fell short to Texas A&M, the Rainbows have accumulated an outstanding home record over the ensuing 26 seasons. One of the largest crowds to watch a Rainbow home football game was October 22, 1988, as 50,089 spectators packed Aloha Stadium to watch their beloved Rainbow Warriors battle Brigham Young University.

Aloha Stadium is a major reason why college football perennial superpowers Notre Dame, USC, Michigan, Texas, Texas A&M, and BYU have all come to Oahu to play against the Rainbows.

NICKNAME: Rainbow Warriors
MASCOT: No Mascot
PLAYING SURFACE: Artificial Turf
SEATING CAPACITY: 50,000
CURRENT HEAD COACH: June Jones
NOTABLE PLAYERS/COACHES: Players: Dana McLemore, Jesse Sapolu, Garrett Gabriel, Jason Elam. **Coaches:** Otto "Proc" Klum, Dick Tomey, June Jones.

Photo credit: Air Survey Hawaii

LOUISIANA TECH

Joe Aillet Stadium (1968), Ruston, Louisiana

Since the 1968 season, the Bulldogs from Louisiana Tech University have compiled an impressive home record inside Joe Aillet Stadium. Named in honor of Joe Aillet, the former Louisiana Tech coaching great, and athletic director, the stadium had an original seating capacity of 23,000. The first game played in the facility took place September 21, 1968, as the Bulldogs led by Terry Bradshaw, crushed East Carolina University 35-7.

The stadium boasts a gorgeous three-tiered press box, a huge and luxurious skybox, as well as two gigantic scoreboards. Louisiana Tech fans, much like the rest of the WAC crowds, are incredibly loyal and loud. Since its opening, Aillet Stadium has been able to house numerous crowds in excess of 20,000. One of the largest crowds ever to witness a game inside the facility took place September 12, 1987, when nearly 25,000 fans watched the Bulldogs battle Northeast Louisiana.

NICKNAME:	Bulldogs
MASCOT:	Champ
PLAYING SURFACE:	Grass
SEATING CAPACITY:	30,600
CURRENT HEAD COACH:	Jack Bicknell

NOTABLE PLAYERS/COACHES: Players: Terry Bradshaw, Willie Roaf, Matt Stover, Tim Rattay, Troy Edwards. **Coaches:** Joe Aillet, Maxie Lambright.

NEVADA

Mackay Stadium (1966), Reno, Nevada

Nestled in the heart of the University of Nevada campus, just north of downtown Reno, is the beautiful Clarence Mackay Stadium. Named in memory of John Mackay, a Comstock Mining millionaire, it opened in style as the Wolfpack beat UC Santa Barbara 33-17, in 1967.

Original capacity was 7,500 seats. Mackay boasts numerous features, such as: a contemporary skybox complex which houses close to 50 suites, a new press box, a recently added scoreboard, as well as updated restroom and concession facilities. Surrounding the field is a gorgeous all-weather track.

Nevada's stadium complex goes to great lengths to cater to the fans as well. Wolfpack games are a celebration, and Mackay Stadium helps to enhance fan enjoyment with a number of well-stocked beer gardens and food courts.

Not only does the University of Nevada football program produce exciting teams that play in a gorgeous facility, the Wolfpack fans are also to be admired. One of the biggest crowds to ever witness a Nevada home game took place October 28, 1995, when 33,391 spectators watched Nevada destroy cross-state rival UNLV 55-32.

NICKNAME: Wolfpack
MASCOT: Alphie
PLAYING SURFACE: Fieldturf
SEATING CAPACITY: 31,545
CURRENT HEAD COACH: Chris Tormey
NOTABLE PLAYERS/COACHES: Players: Marion Motley, Mike Oreno, Frank Hawkins, Charles Mann, Tony Zendejas, Brock Marion, Chris Vargas, Alex Van Dyke, Deshone Myles. **Coaches:** R.E. Courtright, Chris Ault.

Photographs courtesy of the University of Nevada

Courtesy of Rice University Athletics Department

RICE

Rice Stadium has been home to the University of Rice football program since 1950. Many spectators, players, coaches, and media personnel believe that Rice Stadium is the prettiest and best overall football facility in the state of Texas, and possibly the WAC.

Built a year removed from Rice's legendary, 1949 Cotton Bowl season, The Brown & Root Construction Co., constructed the facility in just nine months, working tirelessly in 24-hour shifts until the job was completed.

Unlike many other college football venues, it was constructed for football use only. There is no track around the playing field and there are no other sports that use the facility. The most impressive feature of the stadium is the John L. Cox Weight Fitness Center—one of the finest in the entire nation. It is home to the Rice Owl weight room and cardiovascular area. The Stadium also houses the "Owl Club"— the Rice University Sports Hall of Fame.

Lately, the stadium has been home to a number of different teams. For several years the Houston Oilers used the facility, as did rival, University of Houston, Texas Southern University, and the now-defunct Bluebonnet Bowl. In January of 1974, Rice Stadium hosted Super Bowl VIII.

NICKNAME: Owls
MASCOT: Sammy the Owl
PLAYING SURFACE: Artificial Turf
SEATING CAPACITY: 70,000
CURRENT HEAD COACH: Ken Hatfield
NOTABLE PLAYERS/COACHES: Players: Froggie Williams, Joe Watson, Buddy Dial. **Coaches:** Jimmy Kitts, Jess Neely.

SAN JOSE STATE

Spartan Stadium (1933), San Jose, California

Spartan Stadium, situated on the San Jose State University campus, is one of the western United State's oldest college football facilities. Built in 1933, it has been a great home field for San Jose State over the decades. San Jose State's first win in the stadium came in their first game October 7, 1933, when they whipped San Francisco State University 44-6.

Though the SJS football program is generally overlooked by the higher profile Pac-10 schools, the Spartans have always been very tough to beat in their beloved stadium, winning well over 60% of their home games.

On many occasions, more than 25,000 supporters have packed the stadium. The Spartans beat the Fresno State Bulldogs in front of a record crowd 31,218, November 17, 1990. Recently, another huge turnout was on hand to watch the Spartans up-end previously unbeaten, and highly ranked, Texas Christian University.

Though the facility is primarily used for football, it has also hosted motocross events, soccer competitions, monster truck rallies, and rock concerts. In fact, the largest crowd to attend any event at Spartan Stadium was the 37,000 spectators who watched the rock group ZZ Top.

NICKNAME: Spartans
MASCOT: Tiny
PLAYING SURFACE: Grass
SEATING CAPACITY: 31,218
CURRENT HEAD COACH: Fitz Hill
NOTABLE PLAYERS/COACHES: **Players:** Joe Nedney, Jeff Garcia, David Diaz-Infante, Deonce Whitaker. **Coaches:** Bill Hubbard, Dewey King, Jack Elway, Claude Gilbert.

Courtesy of San Jose State Sports Information

SOUTHERN METHODIST (SMU)

Gerald J. Ford Stadium (2000), Dallas, Texas

Few schools in all of college football have the history which the Mustangs enjoy and are currently building upon. The Gerald J. Ford Stadium and Paul B. Loyd, Jr. All-Sport Center is the gorgeous new home for the Mustangs football team.

The stadium bears the name of Gerald J. Ford, who donated an incredible $20-million to construct the current stadium. It has a capacity of 32,000 seats but can easily increase to over 45,000.

The field itself is situated twenty-five feet below ground level, as is most of the seating. This obviously was done out of respect for the city patrons and Dallas' city noise ordinances. The facility was also designed to hold a regulation-size soccer field in hopes of hosting matches during the 2012 Olympics (assuming Dallas gets the bid).

The venue is home to a huge and very contemporary press box which houses club level seats, along with close to 20 luxury box suites. Other amenities include permanent lights, a gorgeous grass field, and the Paul B. Loyd, Jr. All-Sports Center—so named after former SMU football player and captain, Paul B. Loyd, Jr. It is the jewel of the multi-purpose sports facility, and is home to sports offices, an immaculate weight room area, as well as a number of locker rooms for multiple sports. The Altshuler Learning Enhancement Center also resides in the Center.

The Mustangs had a previous and more famous, home, the Cotton Bowl. The Mustangs played at the Cotton Bowl from 1948 through the 1978 season and were completely dominant.

NICKNAME: Mustangs
MASCOT: Peruna
PLAYING SURFACE: Grass
SEATING CAPACITY: 32,000
CURRENT HEAD COACH: Phil Bennett
NOTABLE PLAYERS/COACHES: Players: Doak Walker, Kyle Rote, Don Meredith, Eric Dickerson, Craig James. **Coaches:** Matty Bell, Hayden Fry, Bobby Collins.

Autumn's Cathedrals 133

TEXAS-EL PASO

Sun Bowl (1963), El Paso, Texas

The Sun Bowl is one of the most recognizable landmarks in the city of El Paso, and is also home to the University of Texas-El Paso football team. Built in 1963, with a seating capacity of 30,000, the Sun Bowl has hosted a number of high-profile events such as rock concerts, NFL scrimmages, monster truck rallies, and world-class boxing matches. Every December, it hosts the annual Sun Bowl football game.

The home of the Miners is an impressive combination of traditional style and contemporary comfort. The Sun Bowl boasts a sturdy playing field, a permanent lighting system, a spacious press box, as well as Captain's Club box seats.

The UTEP Miners are a very exciting team and their program is on the rise. Throughout the years, the Miners have enjoyed a good and faithful fan base, which has packed the Sun Bowl consistently. With the direction in which the program is going and with the availability of great football players in the state of Texas, it should be no surprise that players will flock to UTEP for the opportunity to play in the historic Sun Bowl.

NICKNAME: Miners
MASCOT: Pay Dirt Pete
PLAYING SURFACE: Artificial Turf
SEATING CAPACITY: 52,000
CURRENT HEAD COACH: Gary Nord
NOTABLE PLAYERS/COACHES: **Players:** Brian Natkin, Lee Mays. **Coaches:** Barry Alvarez

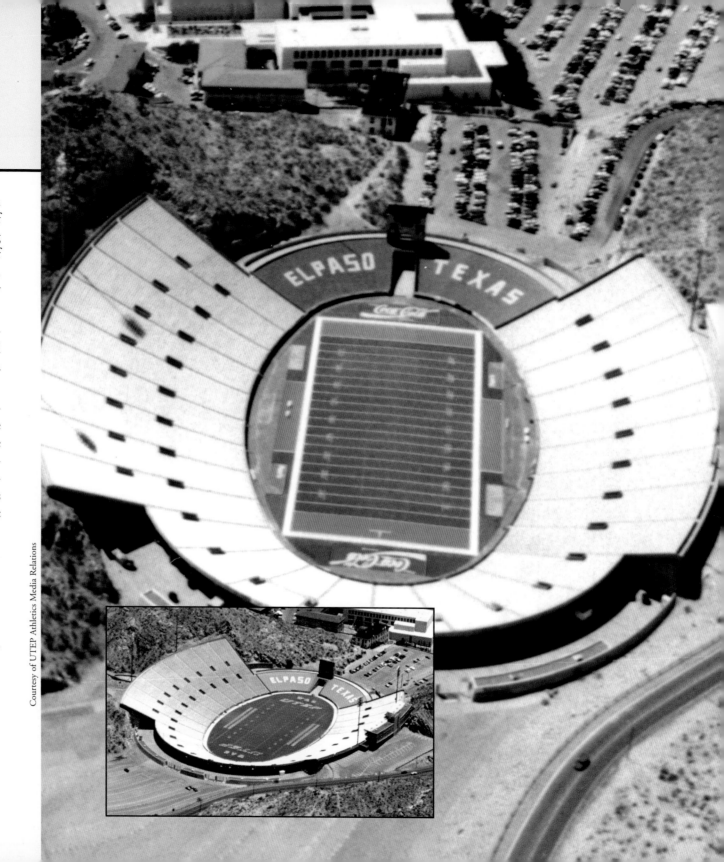

Courtesy of UTEP Athletics Media Relations

TULSA

Skelly Stadium (1930), Tulsa, Oklahoma

The Tulsa Golden Hurricane football team plays its home games at William Skelly Stadium, which was built at a cost of $300,000 in 1930. William Skelly donated almost half of the money to build the stadium and was an avid supporter of the University of Tulsa and the football program. The Golden Hurricane opened the Stadium in grand fashion, beating the University of Arkansas 26-6, October 4, 1930.

Original capacity for the facility was an impressive 14,500 seats. Renovations, improvements, and expansions have not only enlarged the stadium, but also solidified Skelly Stadium as one of the nicest facilities in the WAC.

Fans of the Golden Hurricane program have continually supported their teams. There have been occasions when home crowds in excess of 39,000 have watched Tulsa play, including the time when over 47,000 fans witnessed Tulsa battle the Oklahoma Sooners.

Skelly has hosted a number of other events such as: music concerts, soccer games, and even professional football exhibition games.

NICKNAME:	Golden Hurricane
MASCOT:	Captain Cane
PLAYING SURFACE:	FieldTurf
SEATING CAPACITY:	40,385
CURRENT HEAD COACH:	Keith Burns

NOTABLE PLAYERS/COACHES: Players: Jerry Rhome, Howard Twilley, Drew Pearson, Steve Largent. **Coaches:** Henry Frnka, Glenn Dobbs, Dave Rader.

Directory of Schools

University	Conference	Page #
Air Force	Mountain West	82
Akron	Mid-American (East)	68
Alabama	Southeastern (West)	110
Alabama-Birmingham (UAB)	USA	48
Arizona	Pacific Ten	92
Arizona State	Pacific Ten	93
Arkansas	Southeastern (West)	111
Arkansas State	Sun Belt	118
Army	USA	49
Auburn	Southeastern (West)	112
Ball State	Mid-American (West)	75
Baylor	Big Twelve (South)	40
Boise State	Western Athletic	126
Boston College	Big East	12
Bowling Green	Mid-American (East) *(Moved to West)	69
Brigham Young	Mountain West	83
Buffalo	Mid-American (East)	70
California (Berkeley)	Pacific Ten	94
Central Florida	Independents *(Moved to MAC)	60
Central Michigan	Mid-American (West)	76
Cincinnati	USA	50
Clemson	Atlantic Coast	2
Colorado	Big Twelve (North)	34
Colorado State	Mountain West	84
Connecticut	Independents	61
Duke	Atlantic Coast	3
East Carolina	USA	51
Eastern Michigan	Mid-American (West)	77
Florida	Southeastern (East)	104
Florida State	Atlantic Coast	4
Fresno State	Western Athletic	127
Georgia	Southeastern (East)	105
Georgia Tech	Atlantic Coast	5
Hawaii	Western Athletic	128
Houston	USA	52
Idaho	Sun Belt	119
Illinois	Big Ten	22
Indiana	Big Ten	23
Iowa	Big Ten	24
Iowa State	Big Twelve (North)	35
Kansas	Big Twelve (North)	36
Kansas State	Big Twelve (North)	37
Kent State	Mid-American (East)	71
Kentucky	Southeastern (East)	106

University	Conference	Page #
Louisiana State	Southeastern (West)	113
Louisiana Tech	Western Athletic	129
Louisiana-Lafayette	Sun Belt	120
Louisiana-Monroe	Sun Belt	121
Louisville	USA	53
Marshall	Mid-American (East)	72
Maryland	Atlantic Coast	6
Memphis	USA	54
Miami	Big East	13
Miami (OH)	Mid-American (East)	73
Michigan	Big Ten	25
Michigan State	Big Ten	26
Middle Tennessee State	Sun Belt	122
Minnesota	Big Ten	27
Mississippi	Southeastern (West)	114
Mississippi State	Southeastern (West)	115
Missouri	Big Twelve (North)	38
Navy	Independents	62
Nebraska	Big Twelve (North)	39
Nevada	Western Athletic	130
Nevada-Las Vegas (UNLV)	Mountain West	85
New Mexico	Mountain West	86
New Mexico State	Sun Belt	123
North Carolina	Atlantic Coast	7
North Carolina State	Atlantic Coast	8
North Texas	Sun Belt	124
Northern Illinois	Mid-American (West)	78
Northwestern	Big Ten	28
Notre Dame	Independents	63
Ohio	Mid-American (East)	74
Ohio State	Big Ten	29
Oklahoma	Big Twelve (South)	41
Oklahoma State	Big Twelve (South)	42
Oregon	Pacific Ten	95
Oregon State	Pacific Ten	96
Penn State	Big Ten	30
Pittsburgh	Big East	14
Purdue	Big Ten	31
Rice	Western Athletic	131
Rutgers	Big East	15
San Diego State	Mountain West	87
San Jose State	Western Athletic	132
South Carolina	Southeastern (East)	107
South Florida	Independents	64

University	Conference	Page #
Southern California (USC)	Pacific Ten	97
Southern Methodist (SMU)	Western Athletic	133
Southern Mississippi	USA	55
Stanford	Pacific Ten	98
Syracuse	Big East	16
Temple	Big East	17
Tennessee	Southeastern (East)	108
Texas	Big Twelve (South)	43
Texas A&M	Big Twelve (South)	44
Texas Christian University	USA	56
Texas Tech	Big Twelve (South)	45
Texas-El Paso (UTEP)	Western Athletic	134
Toledo	Mid-American (West)	79
Troy State	Independents	65
Tulane	USA	57
Tulsa	Western Athletic	135
UCLA	Pacific Ten	99
Utah	Mountain West	88
Utah State	Independents	66
Vanderbilt	Southeastern (East)	109
Virginia	Atlantic Coast	9
Virginia Tech	Big East	18
Wake Forest	Atlantic Coast	10
Washington	Pacific Ten	100
Washington State	Pacific Ten	101
West Virginia	Big East	19
Western Michigan	Mid-American (West)	80
Wisconsin	Big Ten	32
Wyoming	Mountain West	89

Stadiums Listed By Name

Stadium Name	University	Capacity
Aggie Memorial Stadium	New Mexico State	30,343
Aloha Stadium	Hawaii	50,000
Alumni Stadium	Boston College	44,500
Amon G. Carter Stadium	Texas Christian University	44,008
Arizona Stadium	Arizona	56,500
Autzen Stadium	Oregon	41,698
Ball State Stadium	Ball State	22,500
Beaver Stadium	Penn State	106,500
Ben Hill Griffin Stadium	Florida	83,000
Bobby Dodd	Georgia Tech	46,000
Bronco Stadium	Boise State	30,000
Bryant-Denny Stadium	Alabama	83,818
Bulldog Stadium	Fresno State	41,031
Byrd Stadium	Maryland	48,055
Cajun Field	Louisiana-Lafayette	31,500
Camp Randall Stadium	Wisconsin	76,129
Carter-Finley	North Carolina State	51,500
Clemson Memorial	Clemson	81,473
Commonwealth Stadium	Kentucky	65,000
Dix Stadium	Kent State	30,520
Doak Campbell	Florida State	80,000
Dowdy-Ficklen Stadium	East Carolina	48,000
Doyt L. Perry Stadium	Bowling Green	30,599
Dyche Stadium	Northwestern	47,130
Falcon Stadium	Air Force	52,480
Florida Citrus Bowl	Central Florida	70,349
Floyd Casey	Baylor	50,000
Floyd Stadium	Middle Tennessee State	30,788
Folsom Field	Colorado	51,748
Fouts Field	North Texas	30,500
Gerald J. Ford Stadium	Southern Methodist (SMU)	32,000
Glass Bowl	Toledo	26,248
Groves Stadium	Wake Forest	33,941
H.H.H. Metrodome	Minnesota	64,172
Heinz Field	Pittsburgh	65,000
Hughes Stadium	Colorado State	30,000
Huskie Stadium	Northern Illinois	31,000
Husky Stadium	Washington	72,500
Indian Stadium	Arkansas State	33,410
Jack Trice Stadium	Iowa State	43,000
Joe Aillet Stadium	Louisiana Tech	30,600
Jones Stadium	Texas Tech	50,500
Jordan-Hare Stadium	Auburn	85,612
Kelly/Shorts Stadium	Central Michigan	30,200
Kenan Memorial Stadium	North Carolina	60,000
Kibbie Dome	Idaho	16,000
Kinnick Stadium	Iowa	70,397
Kyle Field	Texas A&M	80,650
L.A. Memorial Coliseum	Southern California (USC)	94,000
Lane Stadium	Virginia Tech	51,620
LaVell Edwards Stadium	Brigham Young	65,000
Legion Field	Alabama-Birmingham	82,000
Lewis Field	Oklahoma State	50,614
M. M. Roberts Stadium	Southern Mississippi	33,000
Mackay Stadium	Nevada	31,545
Malone Stadium	Louisiana-Monroe	30,427
Marshall Stadium	Marshall	38,016
Martin Stadium	Washington State	37,600
Memorial Stadium	Illinois	70,900
Memorial Stadium	Indiana	52,354
Memorial Stadium	Kansas	50,250
Memorial Stadium	Missouri	68,174
Memorial Stadium	Nebraska	74,031
Memorial Stadium	Oklahoma	75,762
Memorial Stadium	Texas	80,082
Memorial Stadium	Connecticut	16,200
Memorial Stadium	California	75,028
Memorial Stadium	Troy State	17,500
Michie Stadium	Army	39,929
Michigan Stadium	Michigan	107,501
Mountaineer Field	West Virginia	63,500
Navy-Marine Corps Mem.	Navy	30,000
Neyland Stadium	Tennessee	104,079
Nippert Stadium	Cincinnati	35,000
Notre Dame Stadium	Notre Dame	80,012
Ohio Stadium	Ohio State	101,568
Papa John's Stadium	Louisville	42,000
Peden Stadium	Ohio University	25,000
Qualcomm Stadium	San Diego State	71,400
Raymond James Stadium	South Florida	66,000
Razorback Stadium	Arkansas	72,000
Reser Stadium	Oregon State	35,362
Rice Stadium	Rice	70,000
Rice-Eccles Stadium	Utah	45,634
Robertson Stadium	Houston	32,000
Romney Stadium	Utah State	30,257
Rose Bowl	UCLA	94,000
Ross-Ade Stadium	Purdue	67,861
Rubber Bowl	Akron	35,202
Rutgers Stadium	Rutgers	42,000
Rynearson Stadium	Eastern Michigan	30,200
Sam Boyd Stadium	Nevada-Las Vegas (UNLV)	36,800
Sanford Stadium	Georgia	86,117
Scott Field	Mississippi State	52,000
Scott Stadium	Virginia	61,500
Skelly Stadium	Tulsa	40,385
Spartan Stadium	Michigan State	72,027
Spartan Stadium	San Jose State	31,218
Stanford Stadium	Stanford	85,500
Sun Bowl Stadium	Texas-El Paso	52,000
Sun Devil Stadium	Arizona State	73,656
Superdome	Tulane	69,767
The Carrier Dome	Syracuse	50,000
The Liberty Bowl	Memphis	62,380
The Orange Bowl	Miami	74,476
Tiger Stadium	Louisiana State	91,600
University Stadium	Buffalo	31,000
University Stadium	New Mexico	43,000
Vanderbilt Stadium	Vanderbilt	41,600
Vaught-Hemingway Stadium	Mississippi	50,577
Veterans Stadium	Temple	66,592
Wagner Field	Kansas State	50,000
Waldo Stadium	Western Michigan	30,200
Wallace Wade Stadium	Duke	33,941
War Memorial Stadium	Wyoming	33,500
Williams-Bryce Stadium	South Carolina	82,250
Yager Stadium	Miami (OH)	30,012

Teams Listed By Nickname

Nickname	University	Stadium Name
Aggies	Utah State	Romney Stadium
Aggies	New Mexico State	Aggie Memorial Stadium
Aggies	Texas A&M	Kyle Field
Aztecs	San Diego State	Qualcomm Stadium
Badgers	Wisconsin	Camp Randall Stadium
Bearcats	Cincinnati	Nippert Stadium
Bears	Baylor	Floyd Casey
Beavers	Oregon State	Reser Stadium
Black Knights	Army	Michie Stadium
Blazers	Alabama-Birmingham	Legion Field
Blue Devils	Duke	Wallace Wade Stadium
Blue Raiders	Middle Tennessee State	Floyd Stadium
Bobcats	Ohio University	Peden Stadium
Boilermakers	Purdue	Ross-Ade Stadium
Broncos	Boise State	Bronco Stadium
Broncos	Western Michigan	Waldo Stadium
Bruins	UCLA	Rose Bowl
Buckeyes	Ohio State	Ohio Stadium
Buffaloes	Colorado	Folsom Field
Bulldogs	Louisiana Tech	Joe Aillet Stadium
Bulldogs	Fresno State	Bulldog Stadium
Bulldogs	Mississippi State	Scott Field
Bulldogs	Georgia	Sanford Stadium
Bulls	Buffalo	University Stadium
Bulls	South Florida	Raymond James Stadium
Cardinal	Stanford	Stanford Stadium
Cardinals	Ball State	Ball State Stadium
Cardinals	Louisville	Papa John's Stadium
Cavaliers	Virginia	Scott Stadium
Chippewas	Central Michigan	Kelly/Shorts Stadium
Commodores	Vanderbilt	Vanderbilt Stadium
Cornhuskers	Nebraska	Memorial Stadium
Cougars	Houston	Robertson Stadium
Cougars	Washington State	Martin Stadium
Cougars	Brigham Young	LaVell Edwards Stadium
Cowboys	Wyoming	War Memorial Stadium
Cowboys	Oklahoma State	Lewis Field
Crimson Tide	Alabama	Bryant-Denny Stadium
Cyclones	Iowa State	Jack Trice Stadium
Demon Deacons	Wake Forest	Groves Stadium
Ducks	Oregon	Autzen Stadium
Eagles	Eastern Michigan	Rynearson Stadium
Eagles	Boston College	Alumni Stadium
Falcons	Bowling Green	Doyt L. Perry Stadium
Falcons	Air Force	Falcon Stadium
Fighting Illini	Illinois	Memorial Stadium
Fighting Irish	Notre Dame	Notre Dame Stadium
Gamecocks	South Carolina	Williams-Bryce Stadium
Gators	Florida	Ben Hill Griffin Stadium
Golden Bears	California	Memorial Stadium
Golden Eagles	Southern Mississippi	M. M. Roberts Stadium
Golden Flashes	Kent State	Dix Stadium
Golden Gophers	Minnesota	H.H.H. Metrodome
Golden Hurricane	Tulsa	Skelly Stadium
Golden Knights	Central Florida	Florida Citrus Bowl
Greenwave	Tulane	Superdome
Hawkeyes	Iowa	Kinnick Stadium
Hokies	Virginia Tech	Lane Stadium
Hoosiers	Indiana	Memorial Stadium
Horned Frogs	Texas Christian University	Amon G. Carter Stadium
Hurricanes	Miami	The Orange Bowl
Huskies	Connecticut	Memorial Stadium
Huskies	Northern Illinois	Huskie Stadium
Huskies	Washington	Husky Stadium
Indians	Louisiana-Monroe	Malone Stadium
Indians	Arkansas State	Indian Stadium
Jayhawks	Kansas	Memorial Stadium
Lobos	New Mexico	University Stadium
Longhorns	Texas	Memorial Stadium
Mean Green/Eagles	North Texas	Fouts Field
Midshipmen	Navy	Navy-Marine Corps Mem.
Miners	Texas-El Paso	Sun Bowl Stadium
Mountaineers	West Virginia	Mountaineer Field
Mustangs	Southern Methodist (SMU)	Gerald J. Ford Stadium
Nittany Lions	Penn State	Beaver Stadium
Orangemen	Syracuse	The Carrier Dome
Owls	Temple	Veterans Stadium
Owls	Rice	Rice Stadium
Panthers	Pittsburgh	Heinz Field
Pirates	East Carolina	Dowdy-Ficklen Stadium
Ragin' Cajuns	Louisiana-Lafayette	Cajun Field
Rainbow Warriors	Hawaii	Aloha Stadium
Rams	Colorado State	Hughes Stadium
Razorbacks	Arkansas	Razorback Stadium
Rebels	Nevada-Las Vegas (UNLV)	Sam Boyd Stadium
Rebels	Mississippi	Vaught-Hemingway
Red Raiders	Texas Tech	Jones Stadium
Red Hawks	Miami (OH)	Yager Stadium
Rockets	Toledo	Glass Bowl
Scarlet Knights	Rutgers	Rutgers Stadium
Seminoles	Florida State	Doak Campbell
Sooners	Oklahoma	Memorial Stadium
Spartans	San Jose State	Spartan Stadium
Spartans	Michigan State	Spartan Stadium
Sun Devils	Arizona State	Sun Devil Stadium
Tarheels	North Carolina	Kenan Memorial Stadium
Terrapins	Maryland	Byrd Stadium
Thundering Herd	Marshall	Marshall Stadium
Tigers	Memphis	The Liberty Bowl
Tigers	Missouri	Memorial Stadium
Tigers	Clemson	Clemson Memorial
Tigers	Auburn	Jordan-Hare Stadium
Tigers	Louisiana State	Tiger Stadium
Trojans	Troy State	Memorial Stadium
Trojans	Southern California (USC)	L.A. Memorial Coliseum
Utes	Utah	Rice-Eccles Stadium
Vandals	Idaho	Kibbie Dome
Volunteers	Tennessee	Neyland Stadium
Wildcats	Northwestern	Dyche Stadium
Wildcats	Kansas State	Wagner Field
Wildcats	Arizona	Arizona Stadium
Wildcats	Kentucky	Commonwealth Stadium
Wolfpack	Nevada	Mackay Stadium
Wolfpack	North Carolina State	Carter-Finley
Wolverines	Michigan	Michigan Stadium
Yellow Jackets	Georgia Tech	Bobby Dodd
Zips	Akron	Rubber Bowl

Stadiums Listed By Capacity

Capacity	Stadium Name	University	Capacity	Stadium Name	University	Capacity	Stadium Name	University
16,000	Kibbie Dome	Idaho	42,000	Rutgers Stadium	Rutgers	71,400	Qualcomm Stadium	San Diego State
16,200	Memorial Stadium	Connecticut	42,000	Papa John's Stadium	Louisville	72,000	Razorback Stadium	Arkansas
17,500	Memorial Stadium	Troy State	43,000	University Stadium	New Mexico	72,027	Spartan Stadium	Michigan State
22,500	Ball State Stadium	Ball State	43,000	Jack Trice Stadium	Iowa State	72,500	Husky Stadium	Washington
25,000	Peden Stadium	Ohio University	44,008	Amon G. Carter Stadium	Texas Christian University	73,656	Sun Devil Stadium	Arizona State
26,248	Glass Bowl	Toledo	44,500	Alumni Stadium	Boston College	74,031	Memorial Stadium	Nebraska
30,000	Bronco Stadium	Boise State	45,634	Rice-Eccles Stadium	Utah	74,476	The Orange Bowl	Miami
30,000	Hughes Stadium	Colorado State	46,000	Bobby Dodd	Georgia Tech	75,028	Memorial Stadium	California
30,000	Navy/Marine Mem. Stad.	Navy	47,130	Dyche Stadium	Northwestern	75,762	Memorial Stadium	Oklahoma
30,012	Yager Stadium	Miami (OH)	48,000	Dowdy-Ficklen Stadium	East Carolina	76,129	Camp Randall Stadium	Wisconsin
30,200	Kelly/Shorts Stadium	Central Michigan	48,055	Byrd Stadium	Maryland	80,000	Doak Campbell	Florida State
30,200	Rynearson Stadium	Eastern Michigan	50,000	The Carrier Dome	Syracuse	80,012	Notre Dame Stadium	Notre Dame
30,200	Waldo Stadium	Western Michigan	50,000	Aloha Stadium	Hawaii	80,082	Memorial Stadium	Texas
30,257	Romney Stadium	Utah State	50,000	Floyd Casey	Baylor	80,650	Kyle Field	Texas A&M
30,343	Aggie Memorial Stadium	New Mexico State	50,000	Wagner Field	Kansas State	81,473	Clemson Memorial	Clemson
30,427	Malone Stadium	Louisiana-Monroe	50,250	Memorial Stadium	Kansas	82,000	Legion Field	Alabama-Birmingham
30,500	Fouts Field	North Texas	50,500	Jones Stadium	Texas Tech	82,250	Williams-Bryce Stadium	South Carolina
30,520	Dix Stadium	Kent State	50,577	Vaught-Hemingway Stadium	Mississippi	83,000	Ben Hill Griffin Stadium	Florida
30,599	Doyt L. Perry Stadium	Bowling Green	50,614	Lewis Field	Oklahoma State	83,818	Bryant-Denny Stadium	Alabama
30,600	Joe Aillet Stadium	Louisiana Tech	51,500	Carter-Finley	North Carolina State	85,500	Stanford Stadium	Stanford
30,788	Floyd Stadium	Middle Tennessee State	51,620	Lane Stadium	Virginia Tech	85,612	Jordan-Hare Stadium	Auburn
31,000	Huskie Stadium	Northern Illinois	51,748	Folsom Field	Colorado	86,117	Sanford Stadium	Georgia
31,000	University Stadium	Buffalo	52,000	Scott Field	Mississippi State	91,600	Tiger Stadium	Louisiana State
31,218	Spartan Stadium	San Jose State	52,000	Sun Bowl Stadium	Texas-El Paso	94,000	L.A. Memorial Coliseum	Southern California (USC)
31,500	Cajun Field	Louisiana-Lafayette	52,354	Memorial Stadium	Indiana	94,000	Rose Bowl	UCLA
31,545	Mackay Stadium	Nevada	52,480	Falcon Stadium	Air Force	101,568	Ohio Stadium	Ohio State
32,000	Gerald J. Ford Stadium	Southern Methodist (SMU)	56,500	Arizona Stadium	Arizona	104,079	Neyland Stadium	Tennessee
32,000	Robertson Stadium	Houston	60,000	Kenan Memorial Stadium	North Carolina	106,500	Beaver Stadium	Penn State
33,000	Roberts Stadium	Southern Mississippi	61,500	Scott Stadium	Virginia	107,501	Michigan Stadium	Michigan
33,410	Indian Stadium	Arkansas State	62,380	The Liberty Bowl	Memphis			
33,500	War Memorial Stadium	Wyoming	63,500	Mountaineer Field	West Virginia			
33,941	Groves Stadium	Wake Forest	64,172	H.H.H. Metrodome	Minnesota			
33,941	Wallace Wade Stadium	Duke	65,000	Commonwealth Stadium	Kentucky			
35,000	Nippert Stadium	Cincinnati	65,000	Heinz Field	Pittsburgh			
35,202	Rubber Bowl	Akron	65,000	LaVell Edwards Stadium	Brigham Young			
35,362	Reser Stadium	Oregon State	66,000	Raymond James Stadium	South Florida			
36,800	Sam Boyd Stadium	Nevada-Las Vegas (UNLV)	66,592	Veterans Stadium	Temple			
37,600	Martin Stadium	Washington State	67,861	Ross-Ade Stadium	Purdue			
38,016	Marshall Stadium	Marshall	68,174	Memorial Stadium	Missouri			
39,929	Michie Stadium	Army	69,767	Superdome	Tulane			
40,385	Skelly Stadium	Tulsa	70,000	Rice Stadium	Rice			
41,031	Bulldog Stadium	Fresno State	70,349	Florida Citrus Bowl	Central Florida			
41,600	Vanderbilt Stadium	Vanderbilt	70,397	Kinnick Stadium	Iowa			
41,698	Autzen Stadium	Oregon	70,900	Memorial Stadium	Illinois			

(*Top left clockwise*)
Jason Wolfe along side "Howard's Rock" at Clemson Stadium
Dr. Victoria Gable with "Howard's Rock" at Clemson Stadium
Author's sister/daughter, Shannon Laceby at U of Colorado
Author/Mother Stephanie Wolfe